NEW ART ON PAPER

2

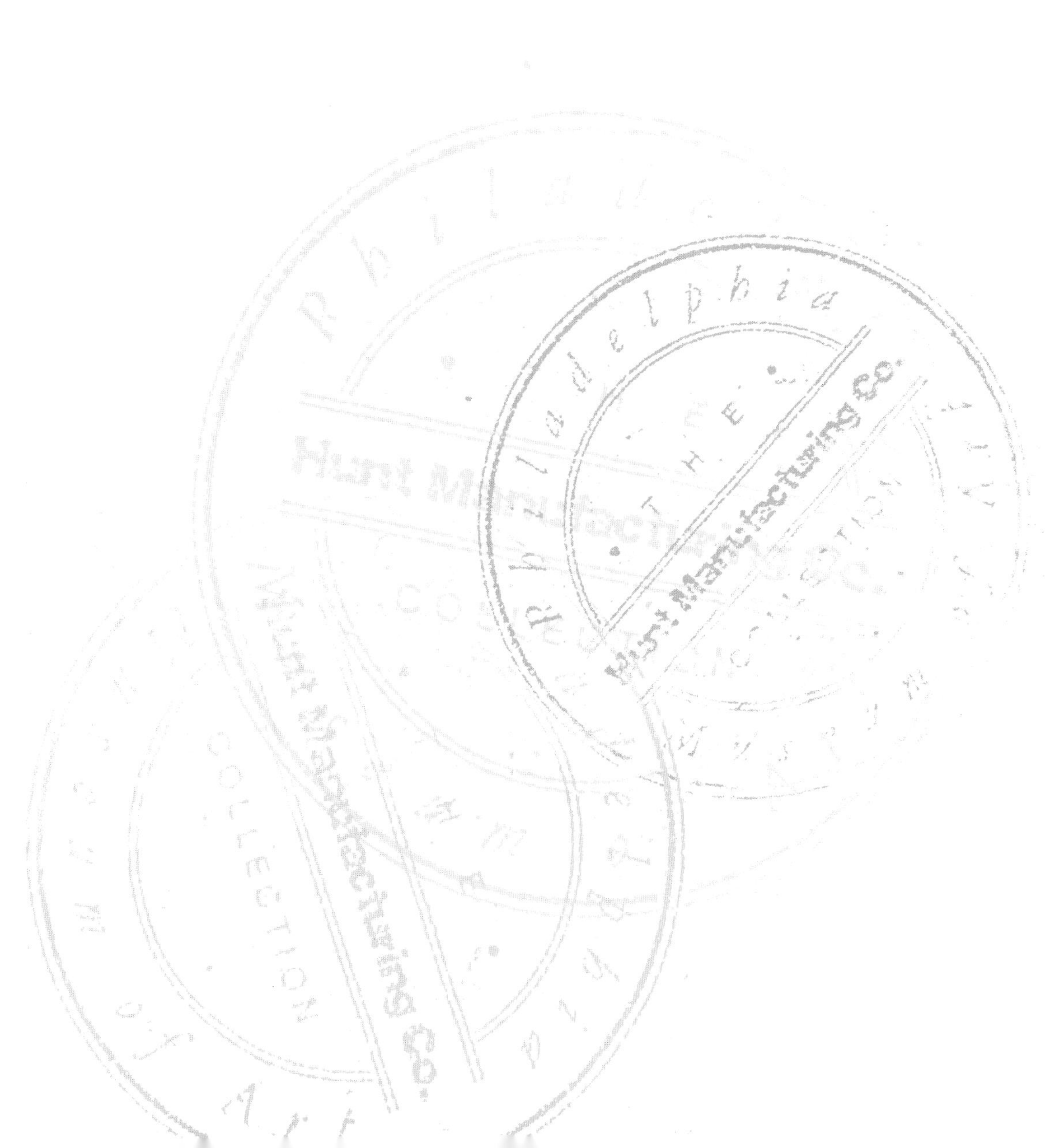

NEW ART ON PAPER 2

Acquired with funds from the
Hunt Manufacturing Co.
1989–1995

Martha Chahroudi
Susan Dackerman
John Ittmann
Ann Percy
Innis Howe Shoemaker

Philadelphia Museum of Art 1996

This book is published on the occasion of the exhibition *New Art on Paper 2, Acquired with Funds from the Hunt Manufacturing Co.*, at the Philadelphia Museum of Art from March 17 to May 26, 1996

The exhibition and this catalogue are made possible by a grant from the Hunt Manufacturing Co.

Edited by Curtis R. Scott
Designed by Phillip Unetic
Production by Sandra M. Klimt
Composition, color separations, and printing by The Stinehour Press, Lunenburg, Vermont

Produced by the Department of Publications and Graphics
Philadelphia Museum of Art
Benjamin Franklin Parkway at Twenty-sixth Street
P.O. Box 7646
Philadelphia, PA 19101-7646

Printed and bound in the United States of America

Library of Congress Cataloging-in-Publication Data

New art on paper 2 : acquired with funds from the Hunt Manufacturing Co., 1989–1995 / Martha Chahroudi . . . [et al.].
p. cm.
ISBN 0-87633-102-9 (cloth)
1. Art, Modern—20th century—Exhibitions. 2. Hunt Manufacturing Co.—Art patronage—Exhibitions. 3. Art—Pennsylvania—Philadelphia—Exhibitions. 4. Philadelphia Museum of Art—Exhibitions. I. Chahroudi, Martha. II. Hunt Manufacturing Co. III. Philadelphia Museum of Art.
N6487.P45P485 1996
709'.04'0074748 11—dc20 96-2426
CIP

CONTENTS

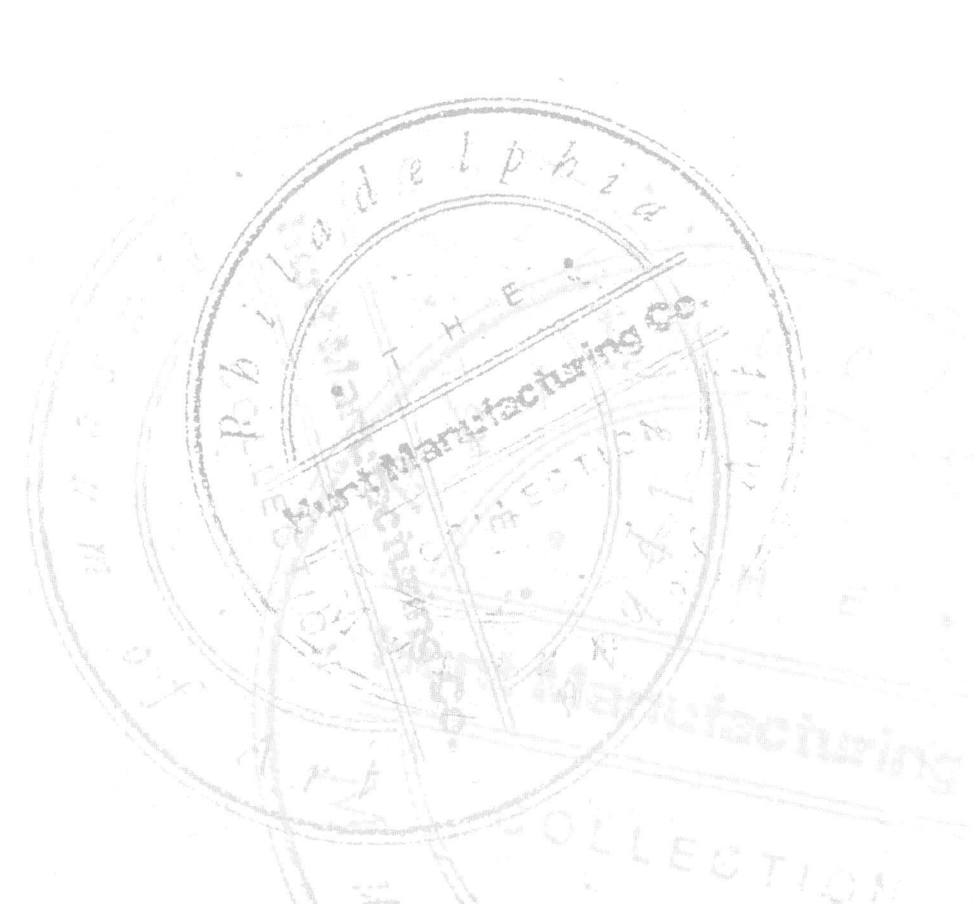

PREFACE

The wild variety of approaches to the making of art encompassed by the works on paper presented in this catalogue bears witness to the happy fact that the quite distinct and traditional skills involved in printmaking, drawing, and photography remain in full and energetic use among artists in the last decades of the twentieth century. They also reveal that any given work of contemporary art is apt to draw on several skills at once, until it eludes conventional categorization altogether. This Museum has reason to be extraordinarily grateful to the Hunt Manufacturing Co. for its inspired insistence on the pursuit of the adventurous in creating the collection that bears its name. Launched in 1979 with an initial grant, the Hunt Manufacturing Co. Collection at the Museum contained works of art by forty-six artists at the time of its first public exhibition in 1988. Since that date, the objects acquired in the first program have settled into their new home and have come to constitute the backbone of the Museum's contemporary collection of art on paper. Hunt's encouragement to widen the scope of the second program by including works that make use of the camera and the computer ensured that the next group of acquisitions would quicken the fast pace set earlier. This exhibition encompasses works of art by thirty-five artists added to the collection over the past six years, and its public debut celebrates the impact of Hunt's initiative upon the life of the Museum.

Many artists in the exhibition "recycle" earlier art or existing images to new purpose, whether they use the computer or the now-venerable Cubist-inspired method of collage. Innis Shoemaker and her colleagues in the Department of Prints, Drawings, and Photographs have risen enthusiastically to the challenge of seeking out works of art that stretch established boundaries of composition or imagery while using techniques that may be centuries old. Conversely, they have also found masterful examples of new technologies deployed in innovative ways, both as a means of reworking earlier images and as tools in creating entirely new works. In the hands of Sherrie Levine, the computer is made to mix and "melt" the primary colors of a Mondrian painting into a perfectly innocent-looking grid of pastels. Kathy Grove uses the more conventional technique of "inpainting" with an airbrush to extract the female figures from a reproduction of Cézanne's *Large Bathers* and fill in the empty landscape left behind, producing an equally radical revision of the past.

In all its diversity, this second installment of the Hunt Collection contains works with a surprising number of elements in common. It emerges as a whole whose parts have the potential to sustain the liveliest of interactions—with each other and with their audience. The presence of several very large, imposing images restricted to black and white, for example, by artists Christopher Wool, Mel Kendrick, and Günther Förg, allows for comparison of radically differing aesthetics within apparently similar formats. A focus on intensely personal, often autobiographical concerns connects diverse artists such as Alison Saar, Paul Thek, and Neil Winokur, while respect for the raw materials and forms of plants in the works of John Cage, Franz Gertsch, and Peter Hutchinson suggests the persistence of artists' interest in nature amidst the attractions of the latest technology.

George H. Marcus, head of publications at the Museum, guided this book into production. Its lively design was provided by Phillip Unetic, and Curtis Scott deftly edited the texts so ably written by the curators and by research assistant Susan Dackerman. Sandra Klimt oversaw the printing of the catalogue, and Graydon Wood and Lynn Rosenthal are responsible for the excellent photographs reproduced herein. The exhibition which this catalogue accompanies has benefited from the thoughtful advice and involvement of Danielle Rice and Glenn Tomlinson in the Division of Education, whose respective contributions of a glossary of graphic arts terminology and an array of quotations from the artists about their work help to make even the most adventurous works of art accessible to all our visitors. The presentation of these new acquisitions inevitably engaged the interest and drew upon the resources of the entire staff of the Department of Prints, Drawings, and Photographs, depending especially upon the skill of preparator Gary Hiatt and the expertise of paper conservators Nancy Ash and Faith Zieske.

Nothing has been static about the Hunt Manufacturing Co. Collection since the late George E. Bartol III, then chairman of the company, first proposed the idea over fifteen years ago. His successor, Ronald J. Naples, was emphatic in his support during his tenure with Hunt, and William Parshall, former secretary of the company's foundation, could not have been more helpful as the initial installment of the collection went on view and the second installment was then launched. We are deeply grateful to everyone at Hunt—most especially to Robert B. Fritsch, president and CEO—for their generous support and enthusiastic endorsement of this exhibition as it has come into being. As the collection has grown apace, with the steady support of the company's board, executives, and staff, it has enriched the Museum, stimulated its curatorial staff, and above all increased the audience for contemporary art by offering visitors and students an opportunity to see recent work within the setting of a comprehensive art museum. The Hunt-sponsored series of annual lectures by artists at the Museum over the past five years won a lively following in Philadelphia, and the works of art themselves can now begin to broaden and deepen that audience as their fresh energy challenges and enlivens all the works of art in the collections they join.

Anne d'Harnoncourt
The George D. Widener Director
Philadelphia Museum of Art

FOREWORD

The connection between corporate philanthropy and the arts, often difficult for businesses to understand, is easier for us here at Hunt to recognize than most. As a manufacturer of art and craft products, our everyday involvement in art leads us to value the art world for its capacity to energize American business and cultural life.

Art not only depends on inspiration—it creates inspiration. Art inspires communication, creative vision, imagination, and innovation—exactly the qualities we at Hunt seek in the men and women who provide our leadership in a highly competitive global marketplace.

When the Hunt Manufacturing Co. Collection began in 1979, it offered us an opportunity to support the Philadelphia Museum of Art in a way that we felt reflected our business attitudes and beliefs, and in a way that these very same business attitudes and beliefs could be expressed in art. The basic and fundamental belief that drives us as a business is that the risk of taking action and the freedom to fail are the necessary costs of making progress. With that in mind, we asked the Museum to acquire adventurous and risk-taking works on paper by emerging artists—works that by definition would not fit many conventional molds. Too often, museums take the course of exhibiting and interpreting works of established historical significance because it ensures an audience. Success is easy when it means dealing solely with what has already gained wide acceptance. The real challenge lies in supporting the adventurous, the controversial, the innovative. Growth and progress originate when an institution or business is willing to move in a new direction, capture a fresh perspective, or engage in a spirit of adventure.

We determined at the outset that the funds we provided would be used toward the formation of a permanent collection of contemporary art on paper. When the collection was first exhibited in 1988, a diverse group of prints and drawings by forty-six contemporary American and European artists represented nine years of judicious collecting by the Museum's dedicated curators. The collection already had a character of its own, distinguished by variety, innovation, and overall high quality.

In 1989, Hunt began funding six additional years of acquisitions for a second exhibition. As before, the Museum had full autonomy to buy high-quality prints, drawings, and photographs by emerging artists whose reputations were on the cutting edge of critical acclaim, rather than works by the most established artists. The curators sought to broaden the scope of the collection by finding works that exemplified the changing nature of contemporary art on paper through the use of new techniques, such as photographic images and processes, and new technologies, such as color copiers and computers—in addition to works that use more traditional mediums in new and innovative ways.

The Museum staff was challenged to build upon their previous achievement and, at the same time, to impart the freshness of perspective evidenced by contemporary artists. Their commitment to searching for the finest representations of contemporary art today is evident in the distinguished works that have entered the collection. The curators are to be commended not only for the exciting results of their efforts, but also for never wavering from the original concept of creating an adventuresome and risk-taking collection. We thank the curatorial staff, the director, and the president of the Philadelphia Museum of Art for their collective wisdom, foresight, and dedication.

Hunt Manufacturing Co. is proud to be associated with this project.

Robert B. Fritsch
President and Chief Executive Officer
Hunt Manufacturing Co.

CATALOGUE

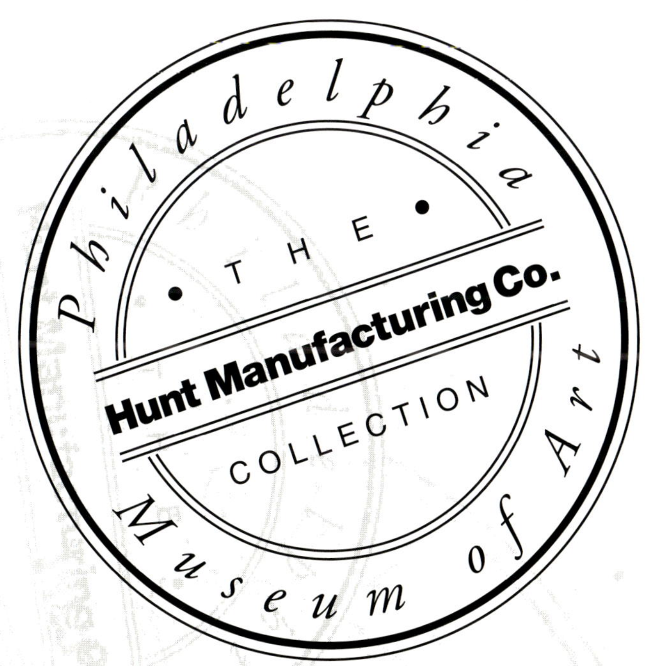
Philadelphia Museum of Art
THE
Hunt Manufacturing Co.
COLLECTION

JOSÉ **BEDIA**

In Kikongo, the language of the Kongo peoples of west central Africa, *ngunda bilongo* means "spell (or influence) of the moon." The dog-man in this enormous ink drawing, trapped by concentric force-lines emanating from the moon, embodies the magic and divination aspects of *palo monte*, the Afro-Cuban religion that José Bedia practices, which combines Roman Catholic and West African beliefs. According to the artist, in ancient Kongo tradition the dog is associated with witchcraft.

Bedia's art is informed by a remarkably consistent intention to reach back beyond the Spanish and African traditions that merged in his native Cuba over the course of four hundred years of European settlement, to establish a connection with the ancient indigenous Indian populations of the island, which were annihilated by the Spanish invaders around the mid-sixteenth century. Bedia is fascinated by aboriginal cultures in general, and he collects artifacts from various societies such as pre-Columbian Mexican, Eskimo, African, Australian, and American Indian. He seeks to tap into a sort of universal quality of primitivism and to conflate this with present-day reality. The simple, strong contours and flat color areas of his drawings and paintings are inspired in part by his long familiarity, from books and from real life, with American Indian pictographs—in 1985 he lived briefly on a Sioux reservation in South Dakota—and in part by the modern cartoon strip.

The paper on which this work is drawn was made from tree bark by the Otomi tribe of south-central Mexico. Bedia likes amate paper for the unforgiving quality of its surface, as one misstroke of the brush or pen on this kind of paper can ruin a work in progress. AP

Ngunda Bilongo (Spell of the Moon)
1991
Black ink on amate paper
47 x 95" (119.4 x 241.3 cm)
1991-147-1

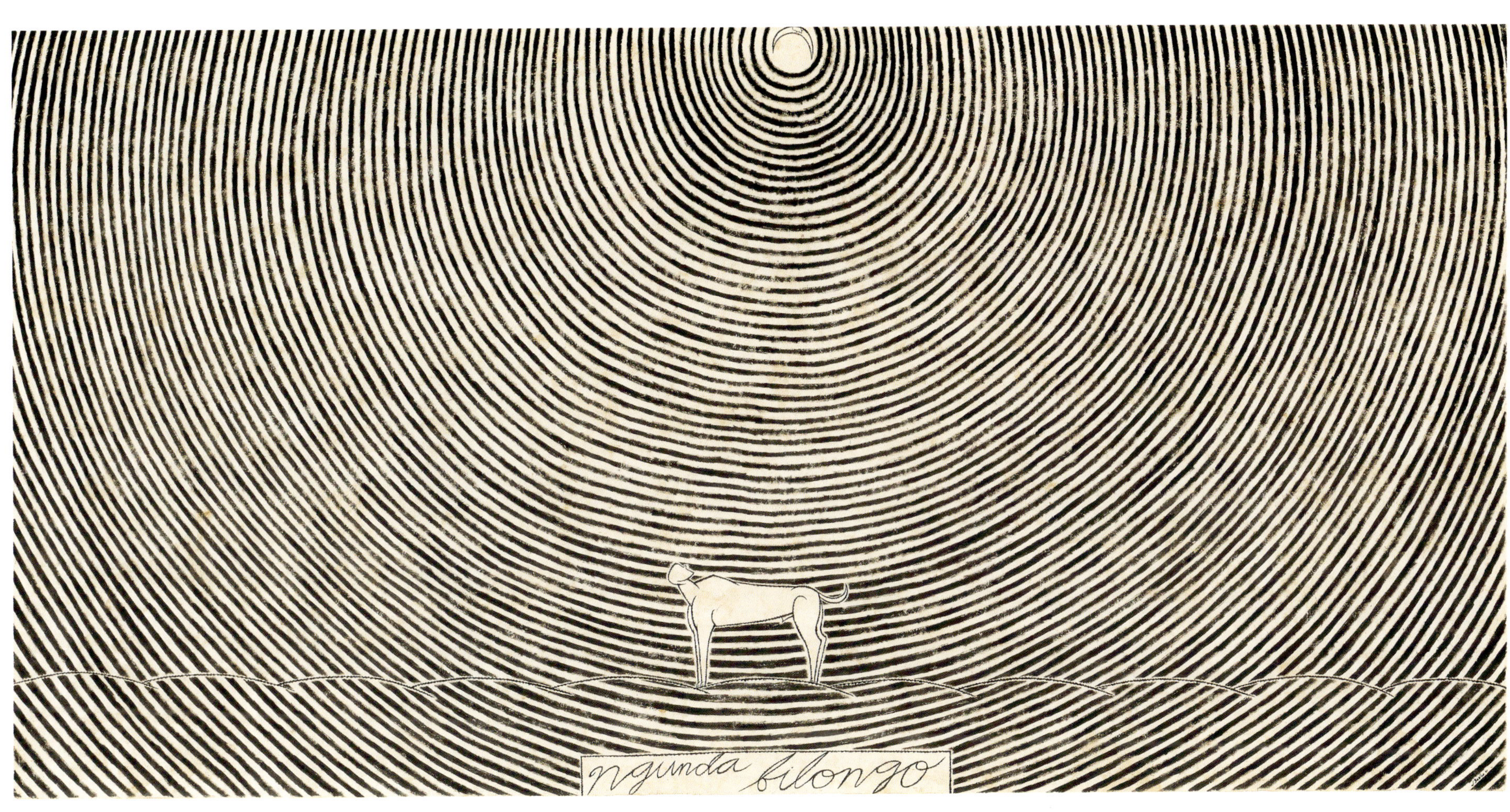
nguinda bilongo

ZEKE **BERMAN**

When William Henry Fox Talbot published *Articles of Glass* in his groundbreaking book *The Pencil of Nature* (1844), with its shelves of symmetrically displayed glassware, he wished not only to show how his new invention of photography could accurately render objects in perfect detail but also to describe, using the already well-advanced science of optics, how photographic materials respond to the material properties of glass in particular. Nearly 150 years later, in *Cans, Triptych*, Zeke Berman, who is deeply interested in both optics and the materiality of objects, reinvented Talbot's photograph from a perspective informed by Gestalt theories of perception and by a modern understanding of photography as being simultaneously representational and abstract.

Although Berman creates his subject within the three-dimensional space of the studio—using bottles, cans, wire, string, and a table against a backdrop of draped cloth—it is the two-dimensional photograph that holds the realization of the artist's intention. He is interested in the dynamic between subject, lens, and viewer. *Cans, Triptych* is a perceptual conundrum which the viewer must puzzle out using the visual clues contained throughout. With continued scrutiny, many elements in the image reveal their physical attributes; others become more conceptual. The viewer must logically reconstruct the image in order to understand what he or she is seeing, and first impressions are constantly challenged in the process. Is the image in two, three, or four parts, or is it a whole? How can a mirror image not be a mirror image? Are objects suspended or supported? *Cans, Triptych* is surely one of Berman's most complex works, yet at the same time, it is an image of restrained and rich elegance. MC

Cans, Triptych
1993
Gelatin silver print; edition 1/20
19 3/4 x 41 1/8" (50.2 x 104.5 cm)
1994-60-1

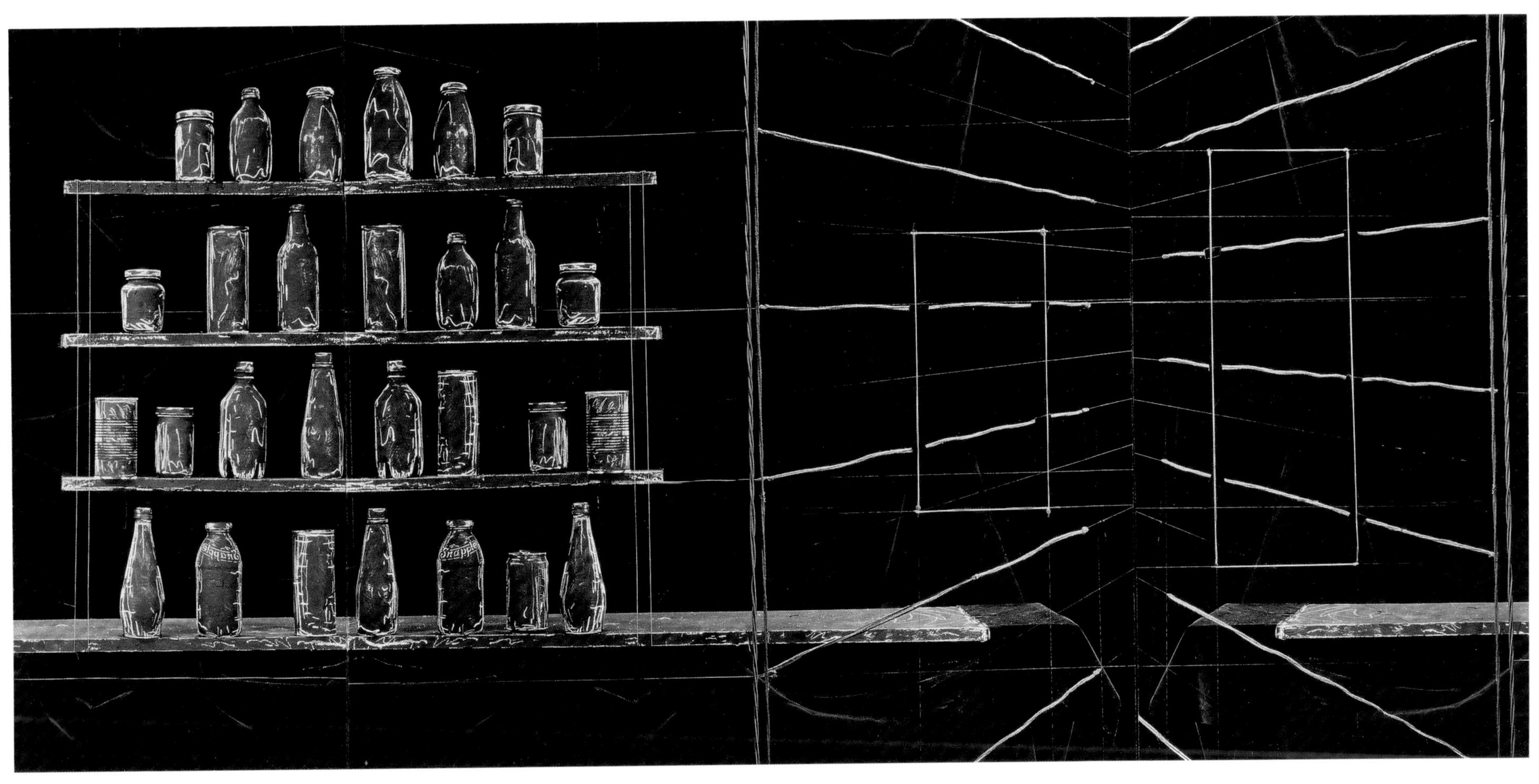

Four Quartets were the first editioned prints Mel Bochner made after a hiatus of eight years, although they have their origins in drawings made in 1982, when Bochner began to use rectangular sheets of paper as building blocks. Similarly, the motif of tumbling cubes on four sheets of paper arranged around a central open square first appeared in charcoal drawings that Bochner began in 1987, after a period of work in Rome.

Bochner turned away from printmaking at a time when his work was concerned with obliterating the concept of picture as object. He claimed that the borders around prints "pictorialized" the image, which made printmaking inconducive to his thinking. In the *Four Quartets*, Bochner finally resolved the border issue by hanging four plates on the wall and working them simultaneously, as he would in painting or drawing. The plates were also simultaneously dipped into the acid. After printing, the sheets of paper were torn to measure fifteen by twenty inches each, thereby eliminating the borders. As in Bochner's contemporaneous charcoal drawings, four printed sheets were arranged around a five-by-five-inch square. Only the *First Quartet* forms a four-sided, square-shaped composition around the central open square, while the other three works are twelve-sided configurations framing open squares at their centers.

The juxtaposition of white lines on black ground in the first and third *Quartets* with black lines on white in the second and fourth, combined with the alternating pairing of vertical and horizontal arrangements of the four sheets of paper that form each composition, together provide a certain mental satisfaction for the viewer, who inevitably becomes involved in figuring it all out. However, satisfied complacence is hardly what these compositions evoke visually. The great tumbling cubes hurtle through space around the open square "eye of the storm," leaving shadows, drips, spots, and linear markings in their wake, and embodying what Bochner aspires to accomplish in his paintings: "I want [them] to feel as if they just exploded into being."[1] IHS

1. Mel Bochner, "Out of Context: Mel Bochner," *Tema Celeste*, vol. 7, pt. 3 (July–September 1989), p. 63.

MEL **BOCHNER**

First Quartet
1988
Aquatint printed from four plates on four sheets of Arches watercolor paper; edition 8/15; printed by Maurice Payne, New York; published by Parasol Press, New York
34½ x 34½" (87.6 x 87.6 cm) assembled
20 x 14¾" (50.8 x 37.5 cm) sheets
1990-4-3

Second Quartet
1988
Sugar-lift aquatint printed from four plates on four sheets of Arches watercolor paper; edition 4/15; printed by Maurice Payne, New York; published by Parasol Press, New York
44¾ x 34" (113.7 x 86.4 cm) assembled
19⅞ x 14⅝" (50.5 x 37.2 cm) sheets
1990-4-1

Third Quartet
1988
Resist aquatint printed from four plates on four sheets of Arches watercolor paper; edition 4/15; printed by Maurice Payne, New York; published by Parasol Press, New York
44½ x 44⅞" (113 x 114 cm) assembled
20 x 14¾" (50.8 x 37.5 cm) sheets
1990-4-2

Fourth Quartet
1988
Open-bite and soft-ground etching printed from four plates on four sheets of Arches watercolor paper; edition 8/15; printed by Maurice Payne, New York; published by Parasol Press, New York
34¼ x 44¾" (87 x 113.7 cm) assembled
19⅞ x 14⅝" (50.5 x 37.2 cm) sheets
1990-4-4

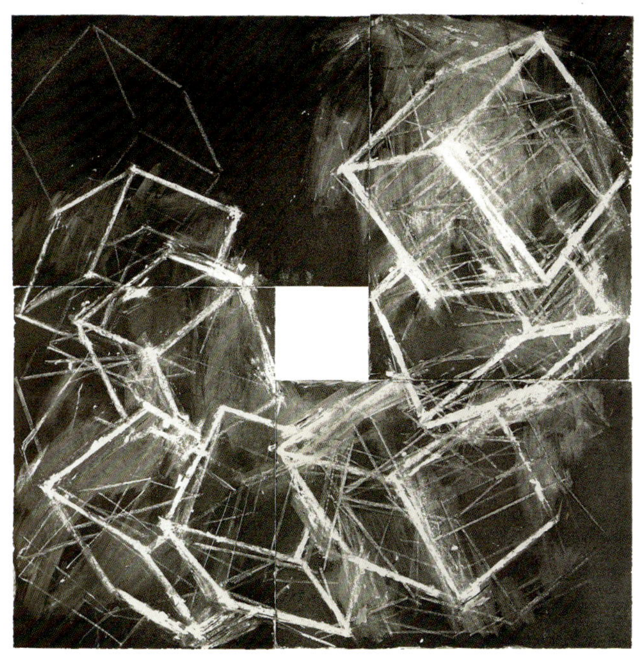

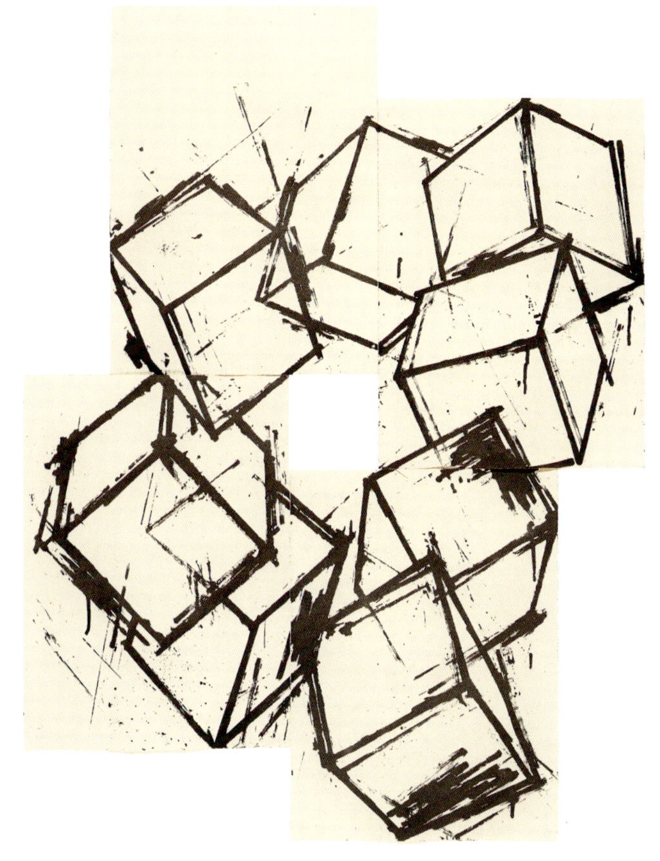

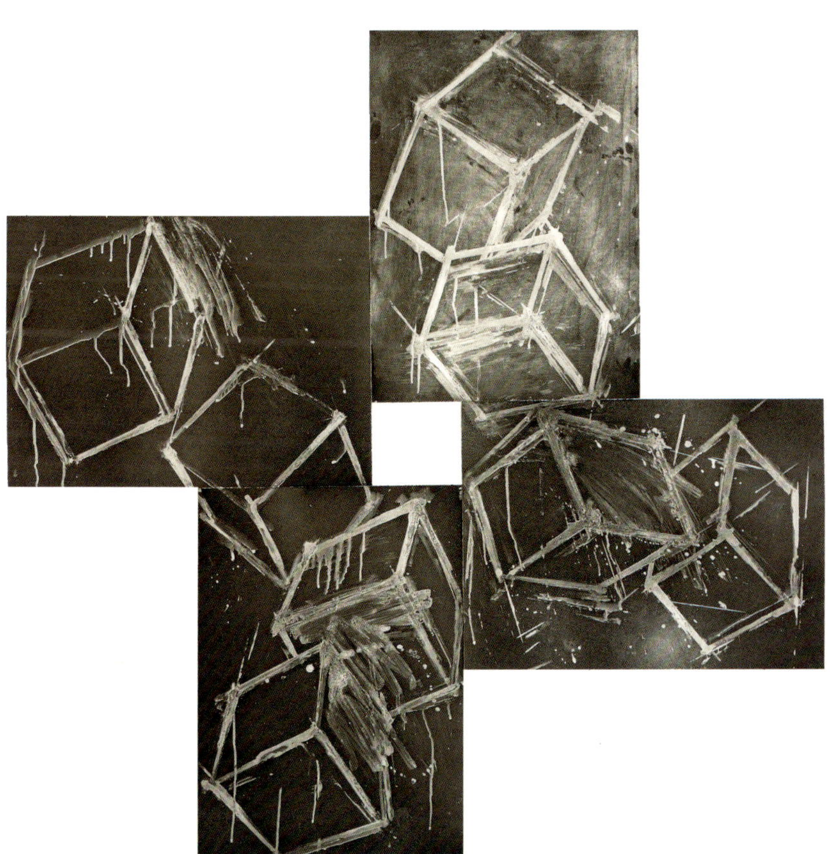

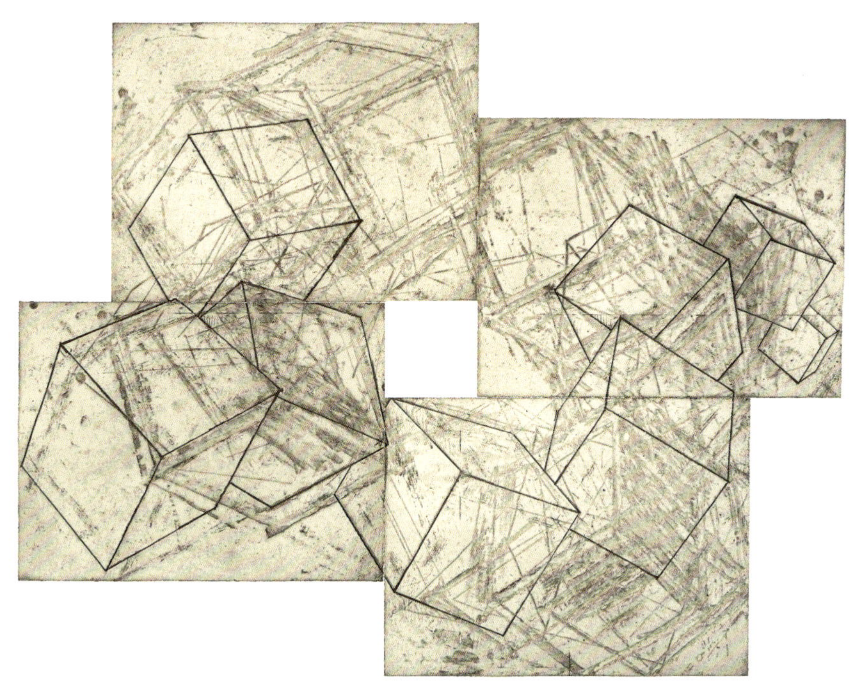

DOVE **BRADSHAW**

Dove Bradshaw has been making carbon removal "drawings" since 1981. To create the pieces, she collects small piles of materials such as dust, hair, wool, tea, herbs, and grass, which she lays onto twelve-inch-wide sheets of sticky tape. After the excess substance is removed, the tacky side of the sheet with adhered particles is placed face down on a piece of carbon paper, ink side up, and carefully rubbed. No effort is made to "direct" the image or to compose the piece: the exposed sticky tape pulls the ink off the carbon paper, and whatever remains constitutes the drawing. The resultant images are elegant, understated, subtle, modest in scale, economical of means, and illustrative of Bradshaw's interest in elusive materials.

In a 1993 exhibition, the artist bound a series of carbon removal drawings in book form and showed them in combination with other, even more essentially indeterminate works that physically change in reaction to their environment. The works shown here are not intended to alter in appearance over time; rather, they conform to Bradshaw's aesthetic of chance and indeterminacy, so closely allied to that of John Cage, in which the distinctions between art and everyday life become blurred by the artist's choosing to create works from objects found around the house and yard—in this case, cooking herbs, tea, and grass. AP

Untitled (Kukicha/Tea),
from the "Carbon Removal" series
1992
Carbon paper mounted on Bristol paper
6⅝ x 5¾" (16.8 x 14.6 cm) image
14⅛ x 11⅞" (35.9 x 30.2 cm) sheet
1994-177-1

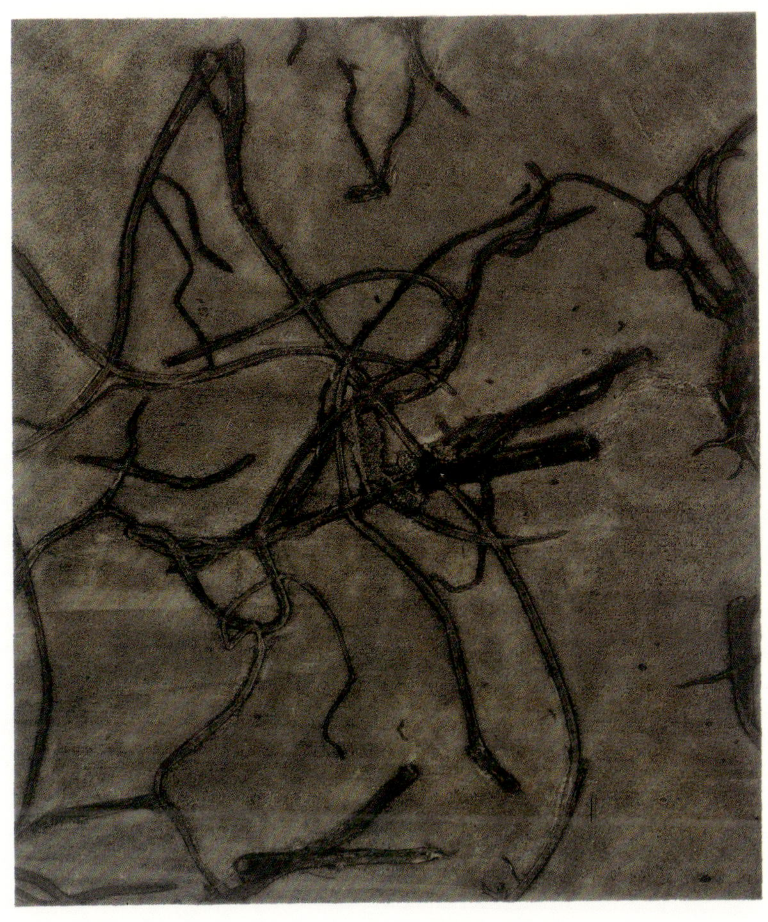

Untitled (Grass),
from the "Carbon Removal" series
1993
Carbon paper mounted on Bristol paper
$6^{3}/_{8}$ x $5^{1}/_{2}$" (16.2 x 14 cm) image
14 x $11^{3}/_{4}$" (35.6 x 29.8 cm) sheet
1994-177-2

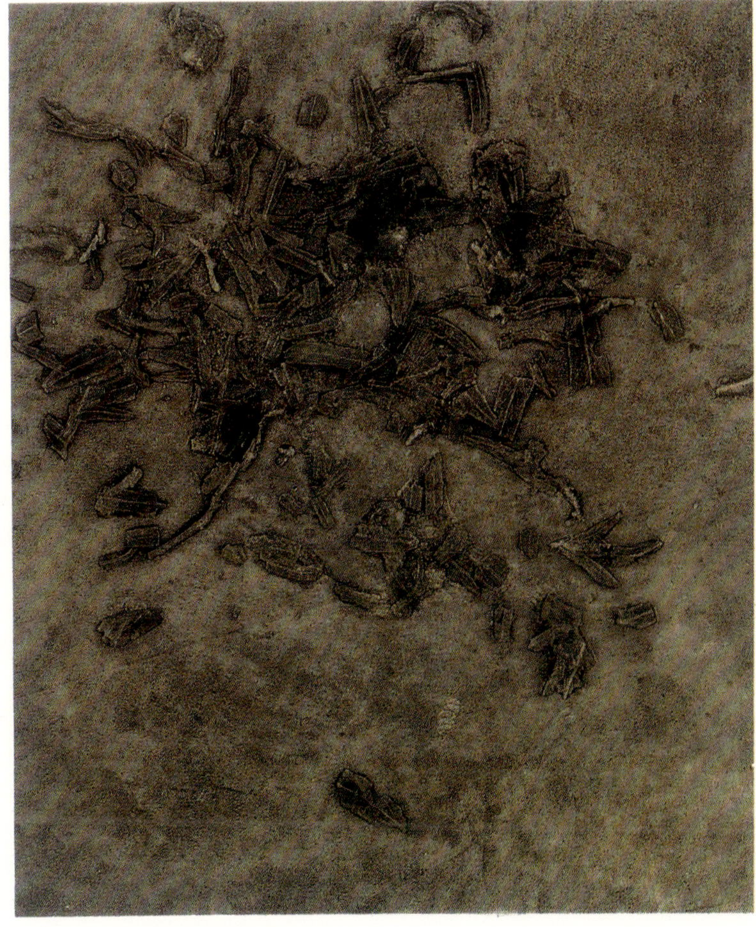

Untitled (Tarragon),
from the "Carbon Removal" series
1993
Carbon paper mounted on Bristol paper
7 x $6^{7}/_{8}$" (17.8 x 17.5 cm) image
14 x $11^{7}/_{8}$" (35.6 x 30.2 cm) sheet
1994-177-3

JOHN **CAGE**

Among the last visual-art works that John Cage produced before his death in August 1992 were three suites of handmade paper pieces created from edible or medicinal plants. In 1989, Bernard Toale and Joseph Zina of Rugg Road Papers and Prints, an experimental papermaking workshop then located in Somerville, Massachusetts, asked Cage to try his hand at making paper. He agreed and chose for his materials the stuffs of the macrobiotic diet he had followed since 1977, procuring ingredients—such as broccoli rabe, mushrooms, ginger root, and Japanese seaweed—from local health food stores. Using only a blender and a papermaking screen, Cage created a suite of twelve handmade papers in an "edition" of two, entitled *Edible Drawings*, in the spring of 1989. The recipes for combining the ingredients were produced through computer charts derived from the *I Ching* (Book of Changes), an ancient Chinese book of prophecy and wisdom.

Beverly Plummer, a musician and papermaker who specializes in working with indigenous plants, had been invited to help with the technical aspects of processing plant materials for the suite, and during the three days of work on that project, the idea arose of creating a second suite from materials gathered in the countryside around Plummer's Burnsville, North Carolina, papermaking studio. In August 1990, after four days of gathering dozens of (more or less) edible plants from the fields and forests—such as hibiscus, mulberry, pokeweed, clover, honeysuckle, stinging nettle, and kudzu vine—Cage produced the suite of twelve papers in an edition of six, entitled *Wild Edible Drawings*, to which the work shown here belongs. The intention was to keep the process very simple—"as close to kitchen art as possible," in Toale's words—by cooking the plants, breaking them down in a blender, and, again, consulting the *I Ching* to develop the recipes.

During this week of work, some of Cage's Chinese medicinal herbs were thrown into the mix, and the idea arose for making a third suite using that type of plant material. Cage obtained the components from a Chinese herbalist's shop in New York's Chinatown, again using the *I Ching* to make the selections from the numerous rows of drawers of herbs and medicines. The painter Terry Winters collaborated on this final suite of twelve papers in an edition of five, which was produced in January 1992 and was entitled *Medicine Drawings*. Small, unpretentious, deliciously textured, and natural as the earth itself, these works are a paradigm for one of Cage's central credos—that art and life are inseparable. AP

Wild Edible Drawing #3
1990
Kudzu, hibiscus stems, cattail, yellow dock, barley, eucommia, and clover; edition of 6
17¼ x 12" (43.8 x 30.5 cm)
1993-15-1

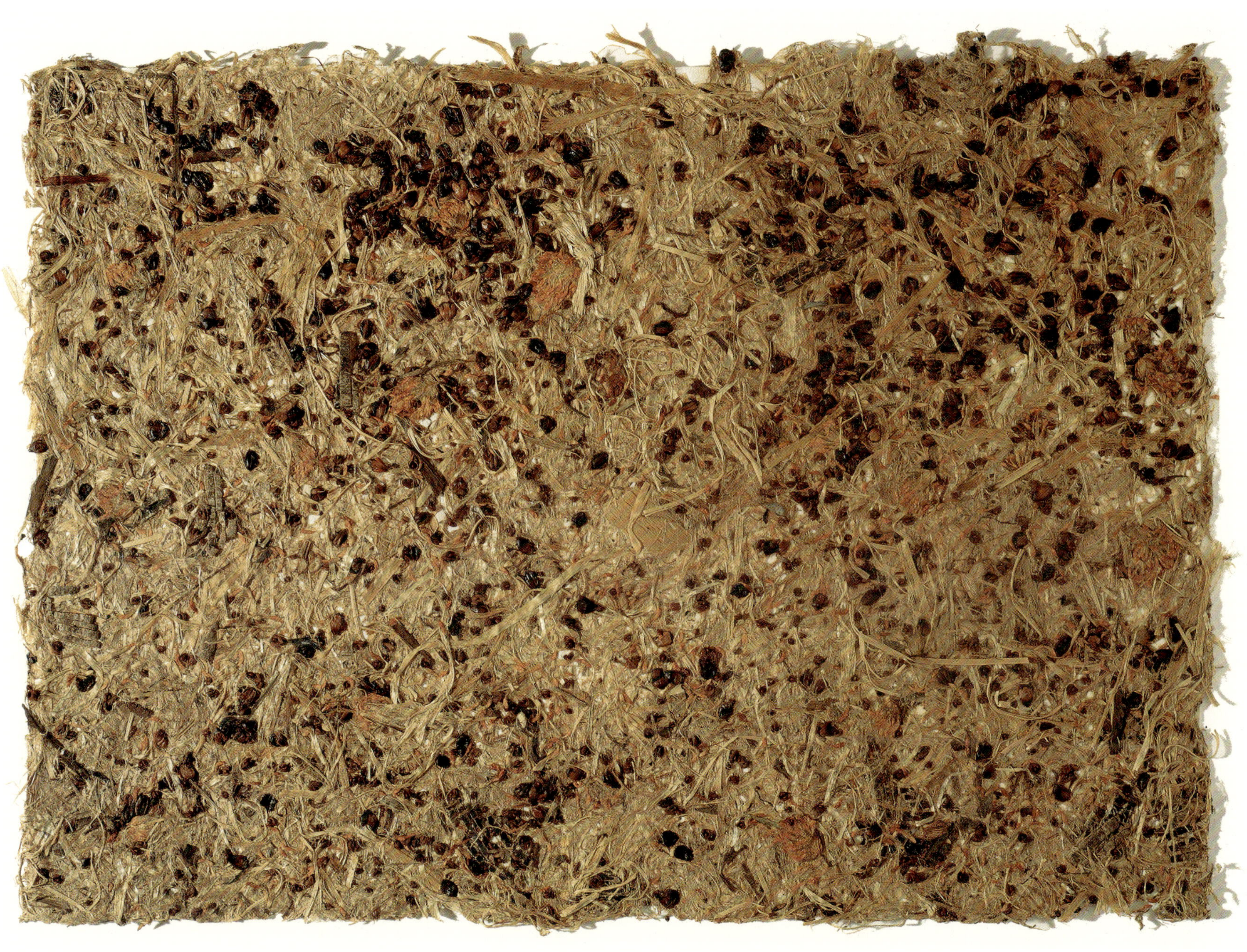

PETER **CAMPUS**

Ironically, when Peter Campus uses the most technologically advanced image-making tool, the computer, to produce his close-up photographs of nature, he controls the construction of the image in much the same way that a painter or a draftsman would. Although he begins with a digitally converted color transparency rather than a blank canvas, he can nevertheless completely reconfigure the forms and colors of his subject, transforming the literal image at will. With Photoshop, a graphics program for Macintosh, he gets to the grain of the photograph itself, its molecular level.

In *burning*, Campus focuses different degrees of attention and uses various types of treatment on different areas of the image. The yew hedge, a backdrop perceived primarily for its function, is naturalistic. The bush also, at first glance, seems to be a literal depiction, though closer scrutiny reveals the artist's hand at work to obscure its precise identity, remaking it as a generic bush to which we can attach the possible symbolism of the title (burning bush). The browned area below the bush, a mulch or a ground that may be completely fabricated, sets the bush apart and emphasizes its central isolation. Finally, Campus creates an obviously computer-generated, uniform pattern of grass, a decoratively mown patch unlike anything seen before in a photograph or in nature! The title *burning* may also be a reference to the common and rather crude darkroom practice of "burning in" an underexposed area of a photograph so as to make it appear uniform with the entire image. In contrast, Campus's techniques are extremely sophisticated manipulations that are hidden or made conspicuous by the choice of the artist. MC

burning
1992
Silver dye bleach print; edition 1/3
$39^{3}/_{8}$ x $50^{1}/_{8}$" (100 x 127.3 cm)
1992-143-1

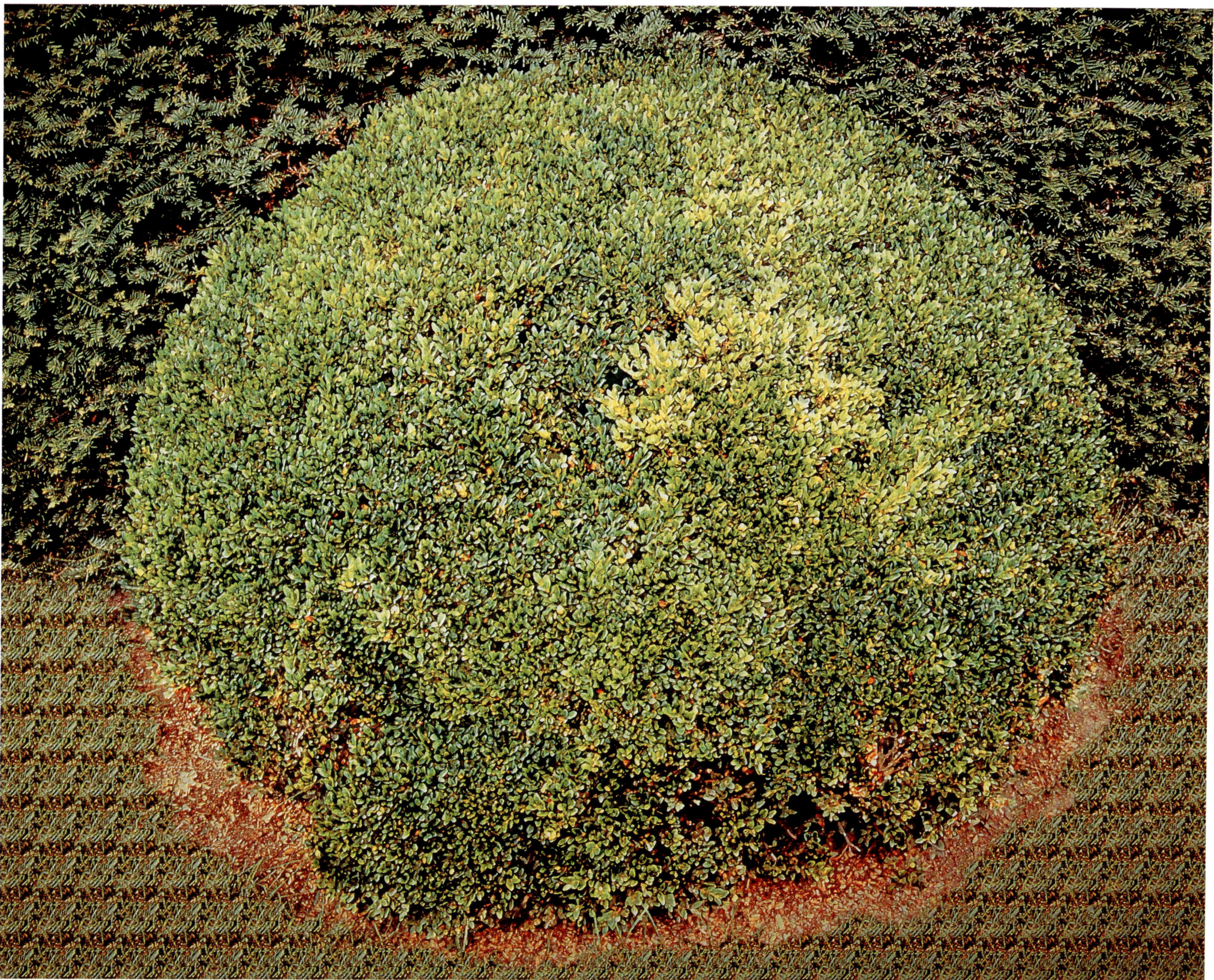

WILLIE **COLE**

Since the end of the 1980s, Willie Cole has created a number of works consisting of scorch marks on paper, canvas, or ironing board covers, in which a pattern is burned into the support with an old-fashioned flatiron; in some instances the works are encased in window frames. The rich, dark tones of the burnt patterns often resemble African textiles, and although they have a highly contemporary look, combining process art and assemblage, the scorch pieces inherently allude to African ritualistic beliefs and activities—such as scarification or fire myths—and to the role of domestic labor, such as ironing, in the African American experience.

Reversed Evidence is one of Cole's "scorches." Full of double meanings and visual puns, it plays on the tension between opposing ideas in the combination of recycled, mass-produced consumer goods—the window frame, pleasantly aged and peeling, that encases the work, and the hot iron used to burn the paper—with the fetishlike aspect of the scorched paper, which has varicolored bits of stuffing material from an ironing board adhered, providing a three-dimensional quality. Cole has said of his scorch pieces: "I like to tap into what I call the spirit in the object: the irons were about heat, so the element in the iron was fire, so I wanted them to suggest fire."[1] In his juxtaposition of American materialism and African spiritualism, of the comfortable familiarity of domestic objects and the ritually or magically empowered fetish, Cole has suggested that he is perhaps unconsciously seeking the African in himself: "I think that when one culture is dominated by another culture, the energy, or powers, or gods of the previous culture hide in vehicles in the new culture. When the Africans came to the U.S. they lost a lot of their cultural icons but the spirits of those icons are hidden in other things."[2] AP

1. Quoted in Elizabeth A. Brown, "Social Studies: 4 + 4 Young Americans," *Allen Memorial Art Museum Bulletin*, vol. 44, no. 1 (1990), p. 15.

2. Ibid., p. 19.

Reversed Evidence
1992
Iron scorches and padding on paper in window frame
33 1/8 x 32 x 2" (84.1 x 81.3 x 5.1 cm)
1993-17-1

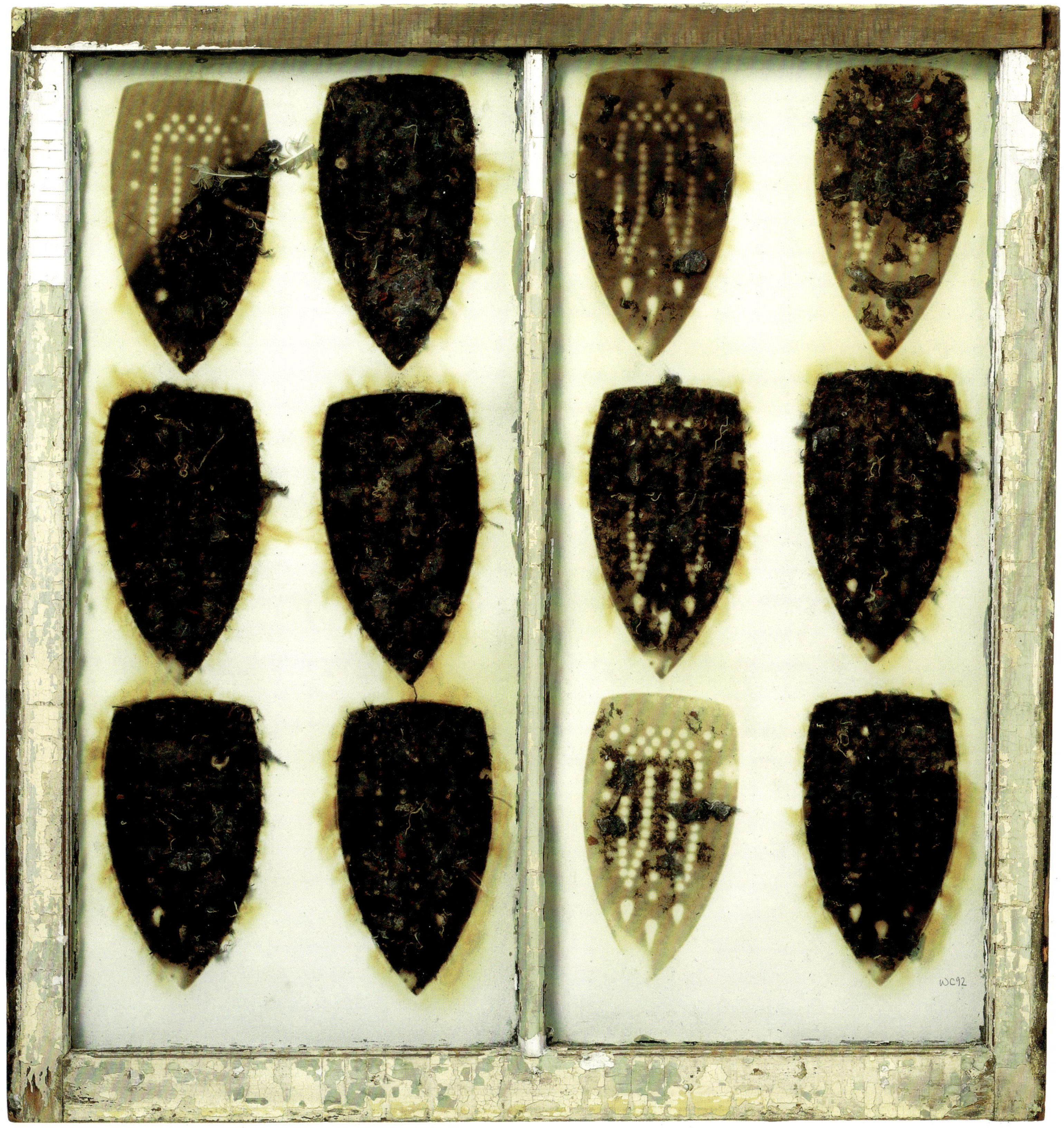
WC92

GREGORY **CREWDSON**

The surface normality of suburban America has fired the imagination of more than one writer or artist. When society has invested so much in maintaining an environment of predictable events and ordinary appearances, a hidden dark side is consequently presumed. John Cheever, Stephen King, David Lynch, Alfred Hitchcock, and Steven Spielberg, among others, have played out the flaws and abnormalities of suburbia in the most bizarre, macabre scenarios. Gregory Crewdson, who acknowledges these mentors, peers into backyards and, somewhat like turning over a rock to find the ground teeming with bugs, discovers very disconcerting things going on there. Animals make fantastic constructions from scavenged materials and act out weird forms of ritual behavior. In this scene, a squirrel stands before an elaborate shrine of berries, half-eaten pears, flowers, cobwebs, and blue Christmas lights with an offering of two dead birds. In other tableaux in this series, robins gather around a primitive circle of eggs, and bright blue butterflies attach themselves to a vertical blind of braided human hair. Of course, Crewdson himself constructs these large-scale scenes in his studio, working for as long as a month in preparation for the final shot. They are natural history dioramas gone awry, densely packed with the creepy detritus of suburbia. Their cinematic potential is accentuated by the brilliant Technicolor hues of Crewdson's prints. MC

Untitled (Shrine with Flowers)
1994
Chromogenic color print, edition 2/6
30 x 40" (76.2 x 101.6 cm) sheet
1995-46-1

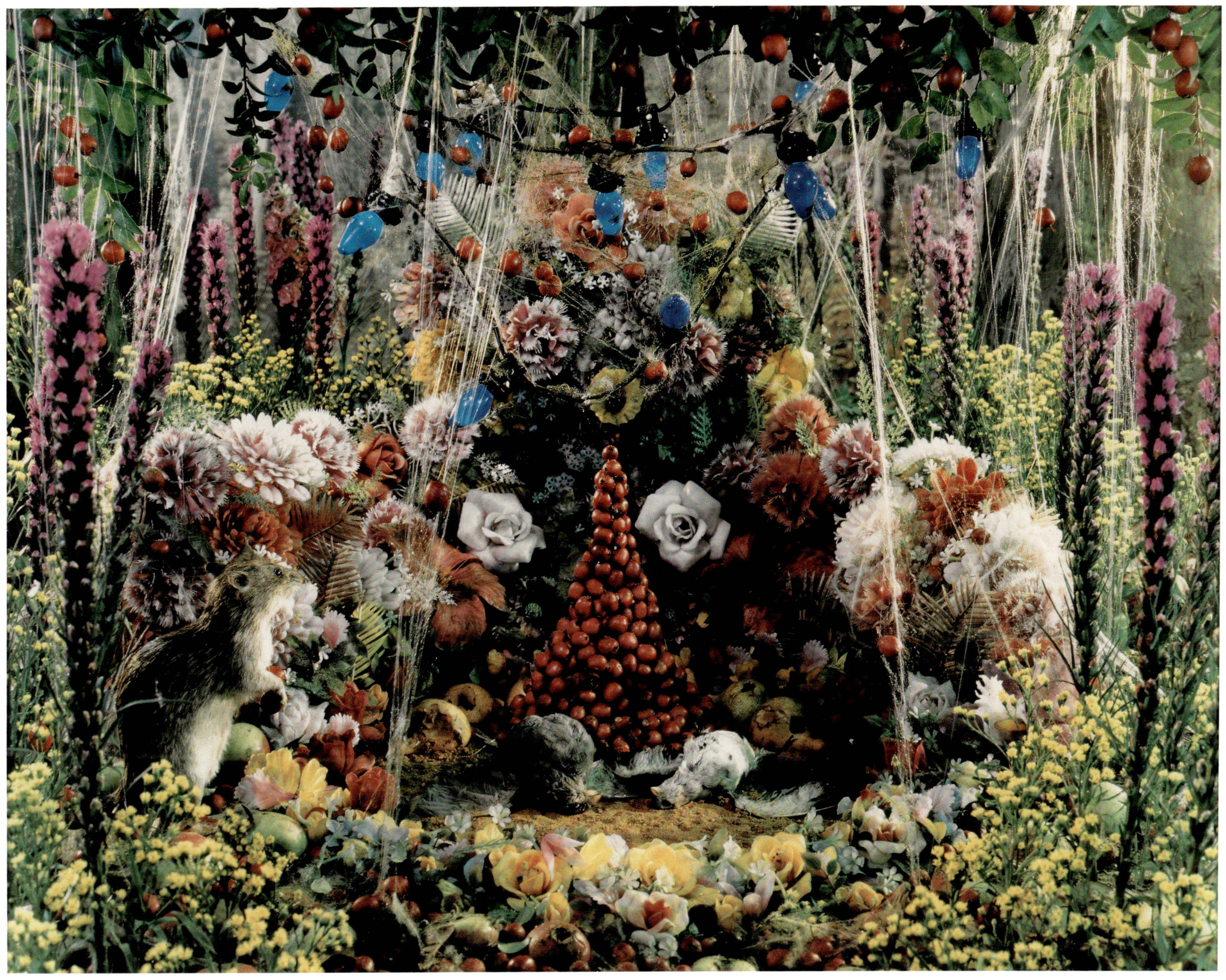

GRENVILLE **DAVEY**

Grenville Davey has called his screenprint series *Eye* "a part, an extension of the sculpture."[1] Superficial evidence of this exists in the title, which Davey has also used for sculptures (*1/3 Eye, Castellated Eye, 3 Minute EYE*), as well as in the circular forms of the objects he chose to use in the prints, which have obvious parallels in the shapes of nearly all of his sculptures. However, the *Eye* series has deeper and more fundamental links to Davey's sculptures, resulting from the artist's use of the computer to explore essentially sculptural, as opposed to printmaking, issues.

The images Davey chose for the prints are actual three-dimensional objects—a glass eye and a glass bottle stopper—which he manipulated on computer in Pair C exactly as though they were sculptures in the round. The objects were first mounted on bases, then photographed and fed into a computer animation program. Davey then moved and shifted the images on the computer screen, eventually presenting them from forty different points of view and in many more relationships to each other; he explored different light effects on their surfaces and played with their shadows. All of these specifically three-dimensional concerns were made possible by computer manipulation of objects and have nothing to do with the traditional representation of images on a flat surface. Even the surfaces of the printed objects were "polished" like sculptures by means of varnish applied selectively to the prints, contrasting the objects with their backgrounds and enhancing the seeming effect of light on their surfaces.

Pairs A and B of the series, which Davey made later than Pair C, are concerned with ways of seeing and as such enhance the significance of the title. The glass eye and the stopper were subjected to two forms of computer analysis. In one view, Davey used a technique called "acute focusing," through which the objects were analyzed in six degrees of close detail, with the result that the more closely they were scrutinized, the more they lost their identities as objects. In the second view of each pair, he produced the same effect but through the opposite means of blurred focus, applying the technique "gauzian blur" to the same six views of the eye and the stopper. IHS

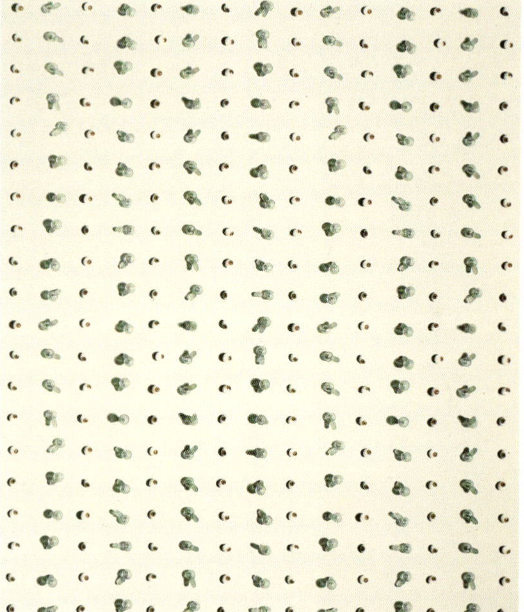

Pair C

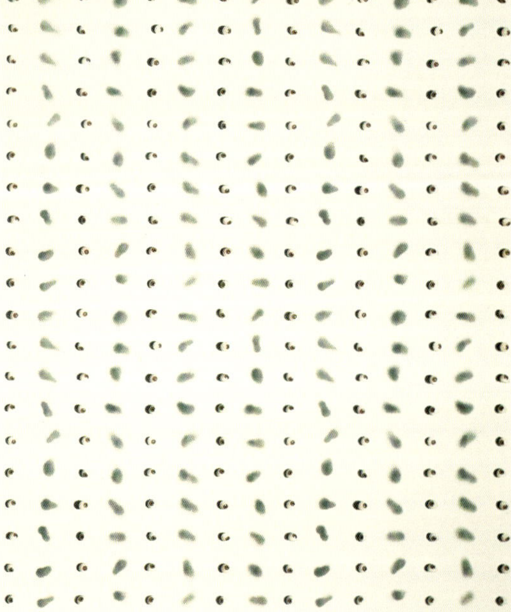

Eye
1993
Six color screenprints on Somerset hot-pressed (satin) paper; editions 32/40 and 33/40 (Pair B, second print); computer work originated with Mark Lucas at After Image, London; printing coordinated by Brad Faine at Coriander Studio, London; published by Charles Booth-Clibborn at the Paragon Press, London
28¹/₄ x 33¹/₈" (71.8 x 84.1 cm) sheets (Pairs A and B)
33³/₄ x 28³/₈" (85.7 x 72.1 cm) sheets (Pair C)
1994-61-1—6

1. Quoted in *Contemporary British Art in Print: The Publications of Charles Booth-Clibborn and His Imprint: The Paragon Press 1986–95* (Edinburgh: Scottish National Gallery of Modern Art; London: The Paragon Press, 1995), p. 74.

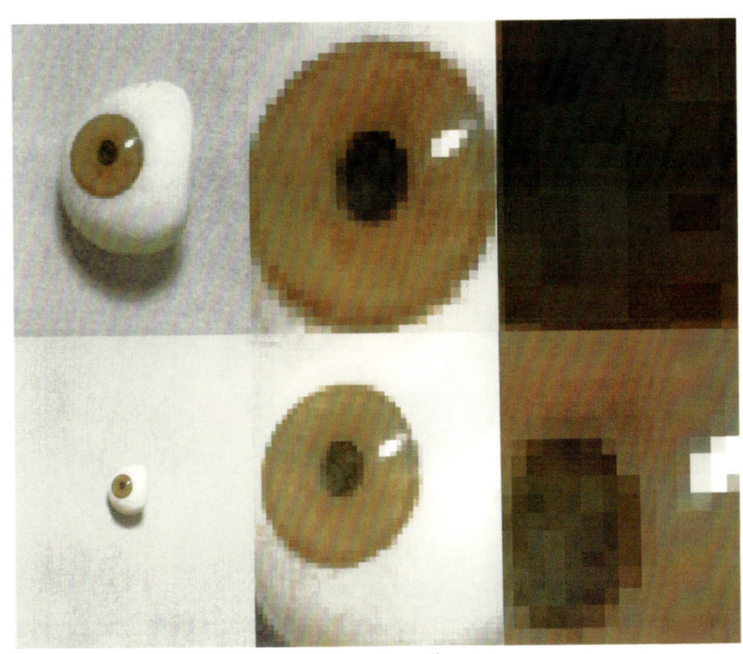

Pair A

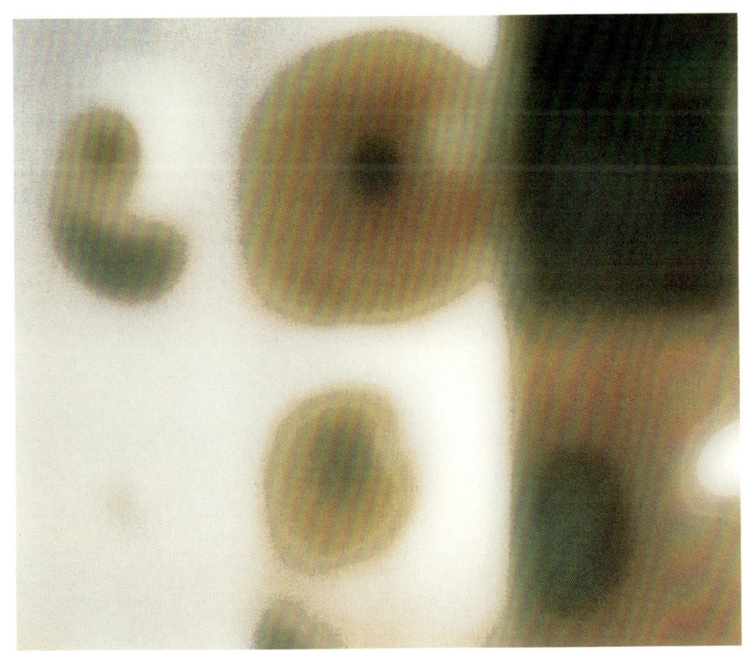

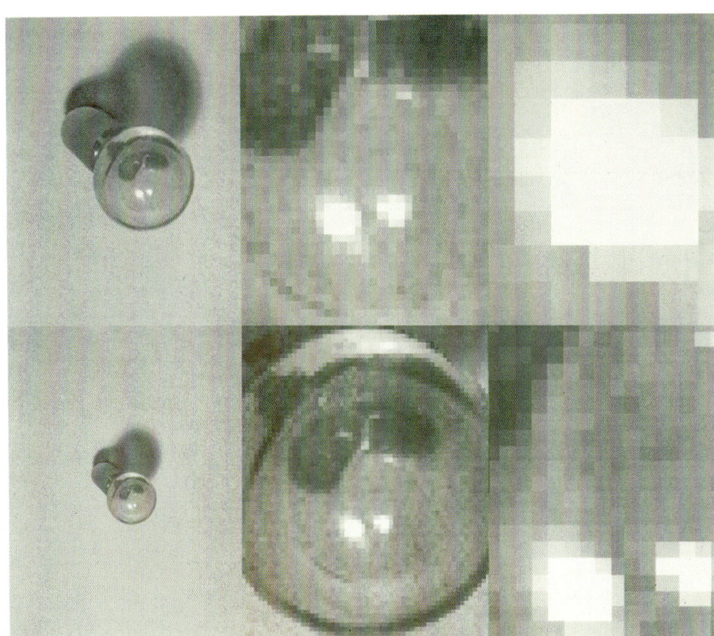

Pair B

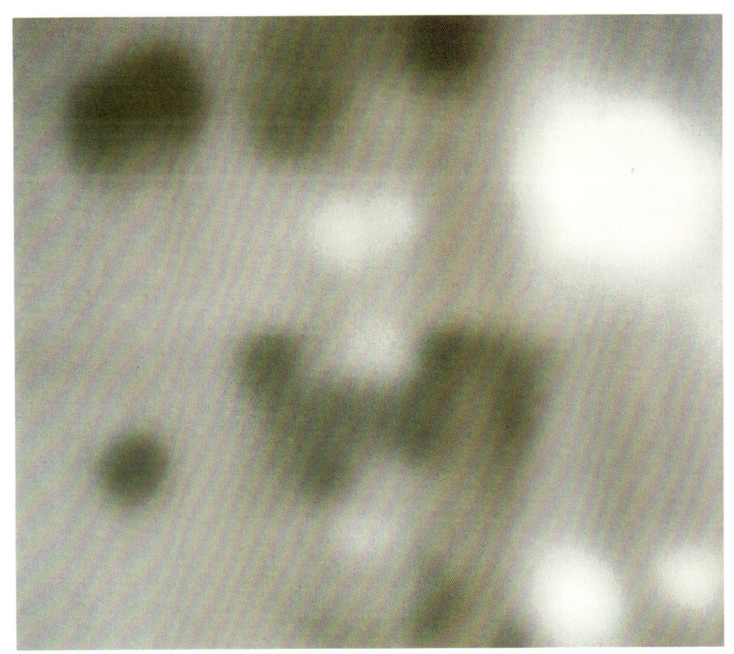

Although they may initially seem closer to Goya's *Caprichos* than to the artist's own sculptures, these two etchings are logical extensions of Richard Deacon's preoccupation with the relationship between conceived and natural forms. Deacon's presentation of oddly grown vegetables as monumental, isolated, humanoid creatures silhouetted against undifferentiated backgrounds may be compared to his conception of his sculptures as entities existing in isolation. The etchings reflect both his fascination with anamorphosis and his motivation, inspired by the poet Rilke, to make objects stand for other things.

The "Curious Potatoes" are two of a portfolio of five etchings that constitutes Deacon's second foray into printmaking. His first series of prints, made in 1987, resembled the biomorphic shapes of his sculptures. This second series of prints, entitled *Portrait*, emanates from an entirely different source: they conflate Deacon's memories of portraits of Victorian public figures with images of freak vegetables illustrated in *Strand* magazine, which Deacon had seen as a child at his grandmother's house and which he had recently rediscovered. By utilizing a complex system of etched hatchings and crosshatchings for the potato "portraits," then isolating them against a smooth, atmospheric, aquatint background, Deacon created an aura of drama reminiscent of grand portraiture, thus explaining the title of the series. IHS

RICHARD **DEACON**

A Curious Potato,
from the *Portrait* series
1992
Etching, aquatint, and polishing on Zerkall paper; edition 16/25; printed by Peter Kneubühler, Zurich; published by Margarete Roeder Editions, New York
39³/₈ x 27⁵/₈" (100 x 70.2 cm) plate
42³/₈ x 30" (107.6 x 76.2 cm) sheet
1992-137-1

Another Curious Potato,
from the *Portrait* series
1992
Etching, aquatint, and drypoint on Zerkall paper; edition 16/25; printed by Peter Kneubühler, Zurich; published by Margarete Roeder Editions, New York
39³/₈ x 27⁵/₈" (100 x 70.2 cm) plate
42³/₈ x 30" (107.6 x 76.2 cm) sheet
1992-137-2

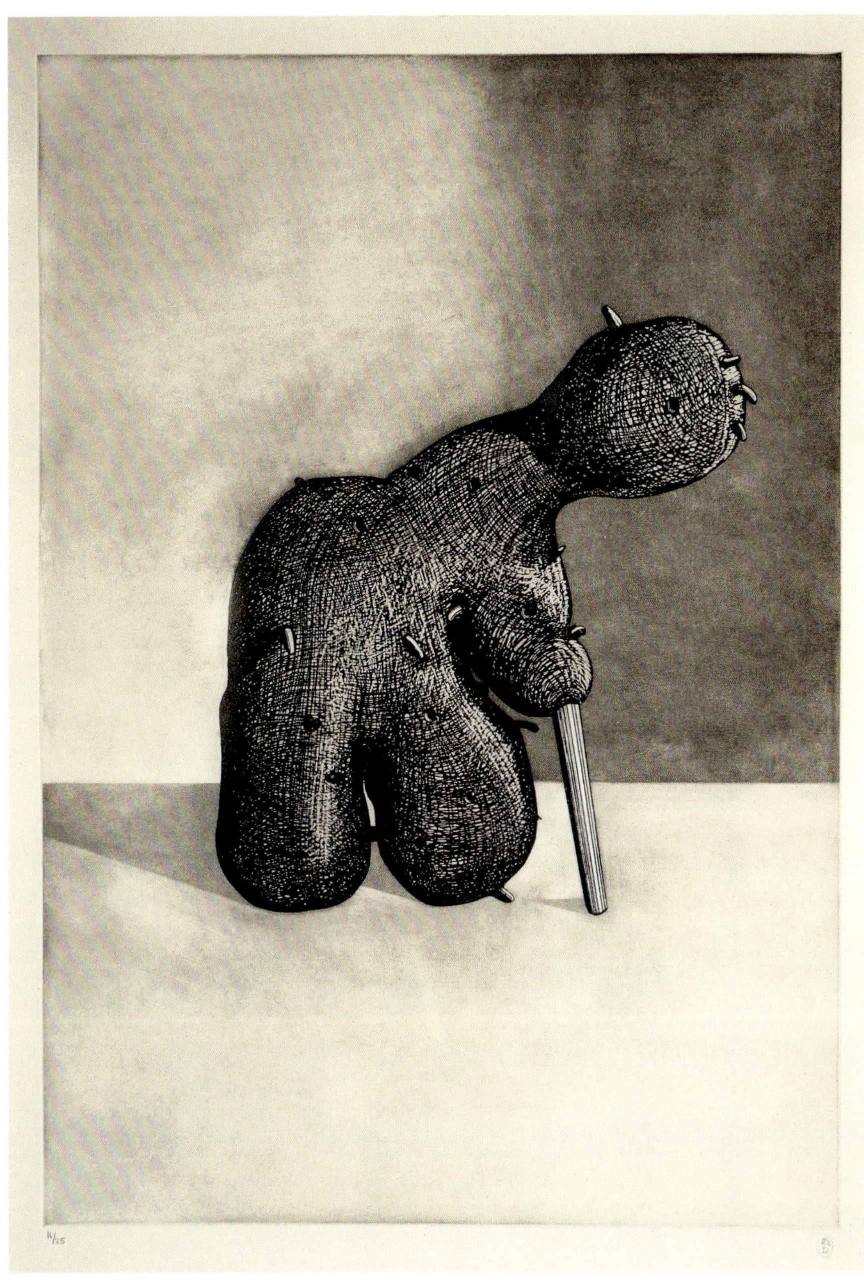

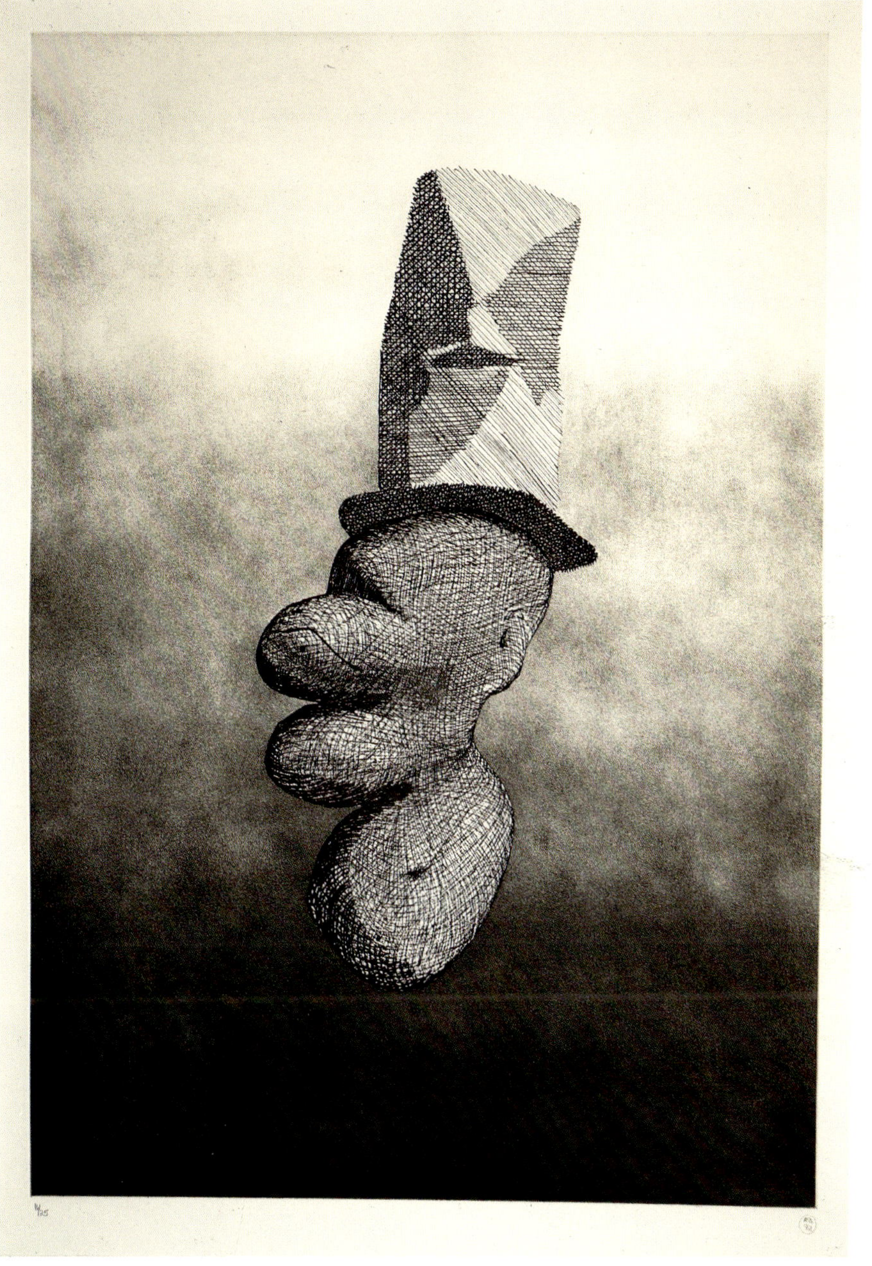

CARROLL **DUNHAM**

Carroll Dunham's interest in science fiction is evident in the alien creatures, objects, and landscapes that pervade his work. His chimerical spectacles are simultaneously likened to the fantastical landscapes of Hieronymus Bosch, the surrealist inventions of Yves Tanguy and Roberto Matta, the psychedelic art of the 1960s, and the late "figurative" work of Philip Guston. Yet for all their affinity with past styles, Dunham's paintings, drawings, and prints still defy explication in many ways. Unlike the decipherable symbols situated within the Boschian landscapes, the entangled forms of Dunham's images are not always immediately distinguishable. And when the shapes and objects are recognizable, their identity, color, and location are often disconcerting: for instance, images of genitalia and stubbly hairs are frequently affixed to mounds of seemingly organic matter painted in lurid and discordant colors. Dunham's personal statements about his work further the ambiguity associated with its interpretation. He has stated that the images he makes are representative of the contents of his mind. The various forms depicted on paper and canvas are the visual equivalent of language, a means to communicate his perceptions of the world in a mode other than speech.

The shapes, lumps, and mounds that populate Dunham's pictures are forms that have evolved over the course of his career, both growing and mutating. The development of the form portrayed in *Point of Origin*, designated by Dunham as "the wave," can be traced through his earlier drawings and paintings. It resembles a gushing mass rising out of a frothy sea, somewhat akin to an erupting volcano or a nuclear mushroom cloud. Dunham's use of multiple and various intaglio processes creates a lush and effervescent surface and enhances the volatile quality of the form depicted. The red and burnt sienna colored inks seem to bubble as they intermingle, and the drypoint, open-bite, and spit-bite markings that surround the exploding form further energize the pictorial field. Dunham has stated that he considers time an integral component in the production of art. The ideas of an artist only fully mature after years of working them out on paper and canvas. *Point of Origin* represents the culmination of several years work and the stunning visual realization of the chaos Dunham's "non-conscious mind is very hungry to see."[1] SD

Point of Origin
1988–92
Color aquatint, drypoint, open-bite and spit-bite etching, and tool work printed from two plates on Echizen Torinoko paper; edition 27/30; printed (by John Lund, Hitoshi Kido, and Craig Zammiello) and published by Universal Limited Art Editions, West Islip, New York
41 x 61" (104.1 x 154.9 cm) plates
49¼ x 68¾" (125.1 x 174.6 cm) sheet
1993-124-1

1. Carroll Dunham, quoted in Carol Eckman, "An Interview with Carroll Dunham," in *Carroll Dunham: Drawings, 1988–1991* (New York: David Nolan Gallery, 1992), p. 12.

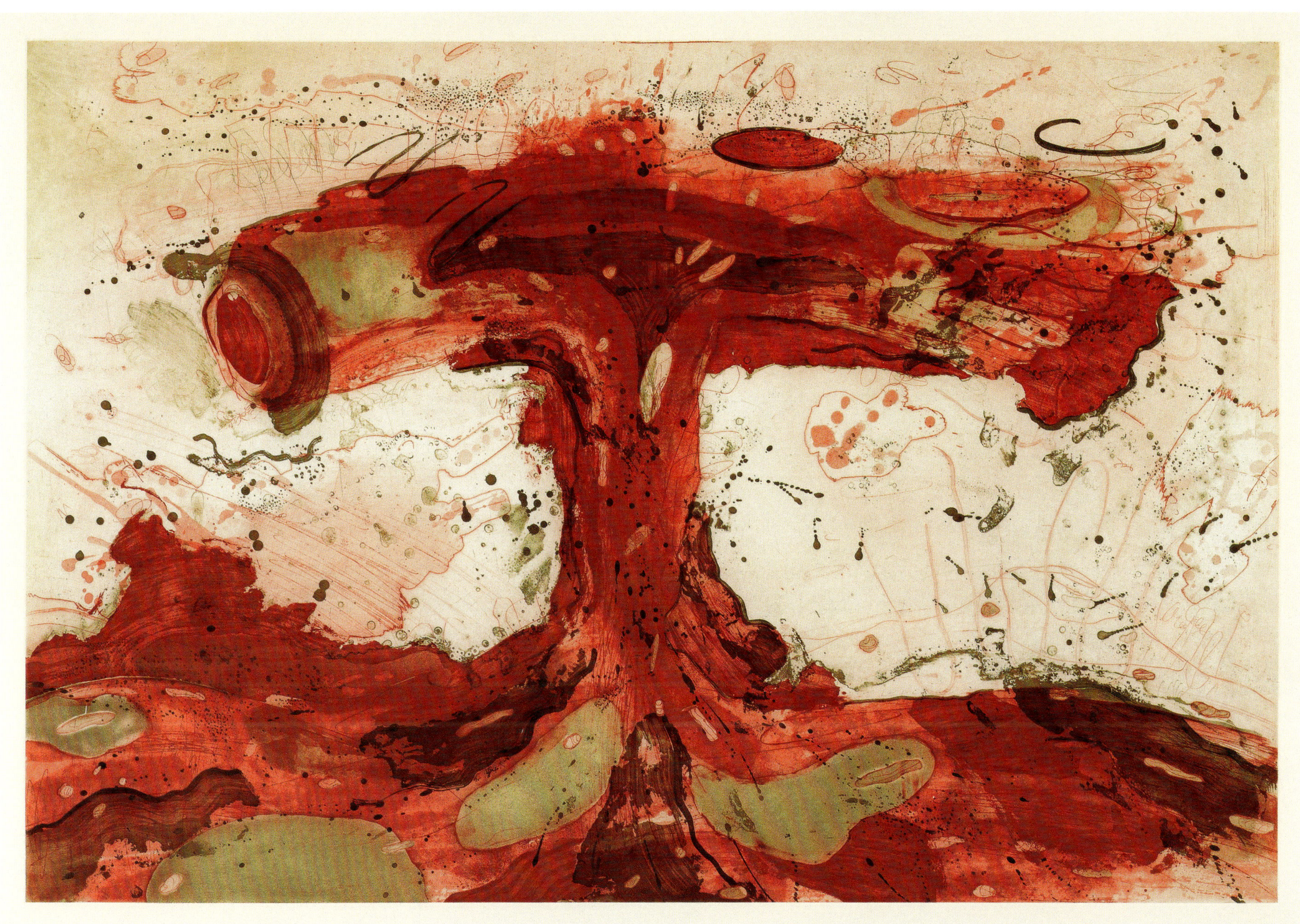

GÜNTHER **FÖRG**

Ragged edges of incised rectangles in Günther Förg's seven-foot-tall print *Untitled* cue the eye that the matrix is metal and that the medium is etching, yet an aquatint grain has been applied to the plate with such sweeping strokes that the printed surface still looks wet and soft. Such visual ambiguity is an essential feature of Förg's work, as can be seen in his cast bronze reliefs, where the malleable appearance belies the obdurate character of the material.

Architecture is a central concern in Förg's art—whether in wall paintings, in the serial placement of his works, or in photographs of actual installations—and is even reflected in the design layout of exhibition catalogues, which frequently include installation photographs along with the images of the individual works. Förg's on-site photographs of such classic examples of Bauhaus architecture as the reconstructed version of Ludwig Mies van der Rohe's German Pavilion, originally built for the 1929 Barcelona International Exposition, capture the play of light on glass, chrome, and marble. When exhibited, these floor-length photographs act as windows onto an outside world, a pictorial device of German Romantic painting. The upright format and double-panel design of *Untitled* allow it to stand doorlike against the gallery wall, endowing it with an architectural role within the room. Under reflective glazing, *Untitled* mirrors the viewer darkly, a calculated effect that Förg considers an essential part of his installations. JI

Untitled
1992
Etching and aquatint on Somerset paper, edition 3/10; printed by Niels Borch Jensen, Copenhagen; published by Maximilian Verlag Sabine Knust, Munich
79 x 39" (200.7 x 99.1 cm) plate
86¼ x 46½" (219.1 x 118.1 cm) sheet
1993-125-1

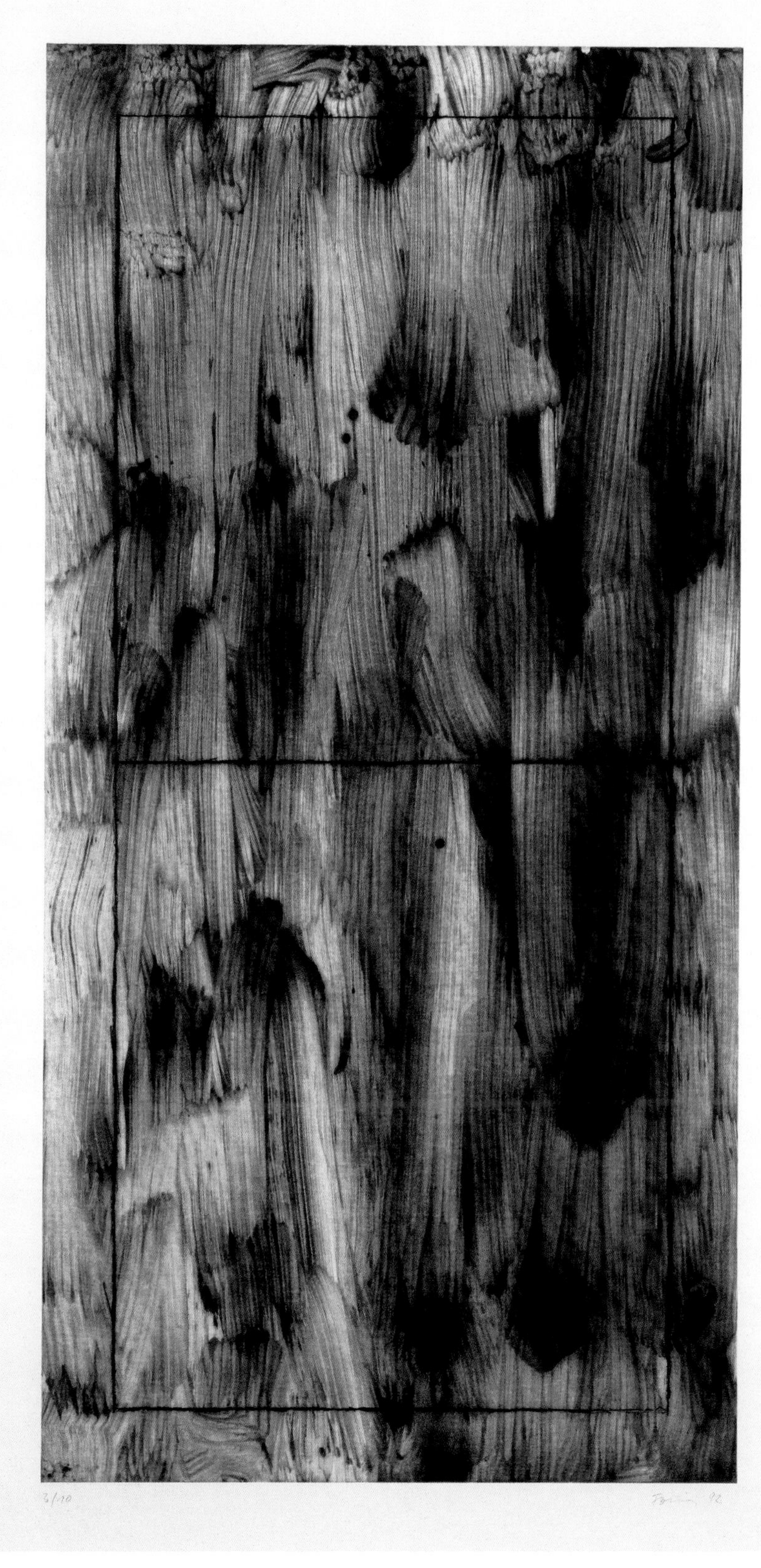

FRANZ **GERTSCH**

In *Pestwurz (Winter Heliotrope)*, Franz Gertsch maps the reticulate surfaces and dentate margins of a botanical specimen, seeming to call forth an entire universe from a single leaf. This blend of scientific observation and poetic vision finds precedent in the nature studies of earlier Northern European artists, from such marvels of the Renaissance as Albrecht Dürer's exquisite watercolors of flora and fauna to the intricate scissorworks of the German Romantic generation, such as Philipp Otto Runge's silhouette cutouts of weeds and flowers.

A painter who now rarely paints, Gertsch works primarily on color woodcuts, hand-inked and hand-printed in small editions on Japanese paper, either in monochrome or in multiple layers of color. The artist brings a reverential, ritualistic approach to the craft of printmaking, mixing his own inks from powdered pigments and using natural substances such as wood ash and charcoal to print dense surfaces of evocative coloration, as here in *Pestwurz (Winter Heliotrope)*. The scale and subject matter of Gertsch's meticulously detailed work range from wall-sized portrait heads to small, close-up views of nature, many of which he frequently prints in different color versions to express distinct sensations. In each case, Gertsch uses projected color slides to guide him as he punches patterns of light into the surface of the woodblock with a sharp gouge. The light transmitted from his slides forms the basis of his vision, since the untouched, reserved surfaces of the block carry the pigment, while the image is revealed as a veil of uninked punchwork dots. JI

Pestwurz (Winter Heliotrope)
1994
Woodcut with charcoal pigment on Japanese Heizaburo paper; artist's edition I/XX; printed by the artist; published by Gesellschaft für den Verein Cerebral Gelähmter Kinder
13 5/8 x 18 7/8" (34.6 x 47.9 cm) block
21 1/4 x 25 1/4" (54 x 64.1 cm) sheet
1994-178-1

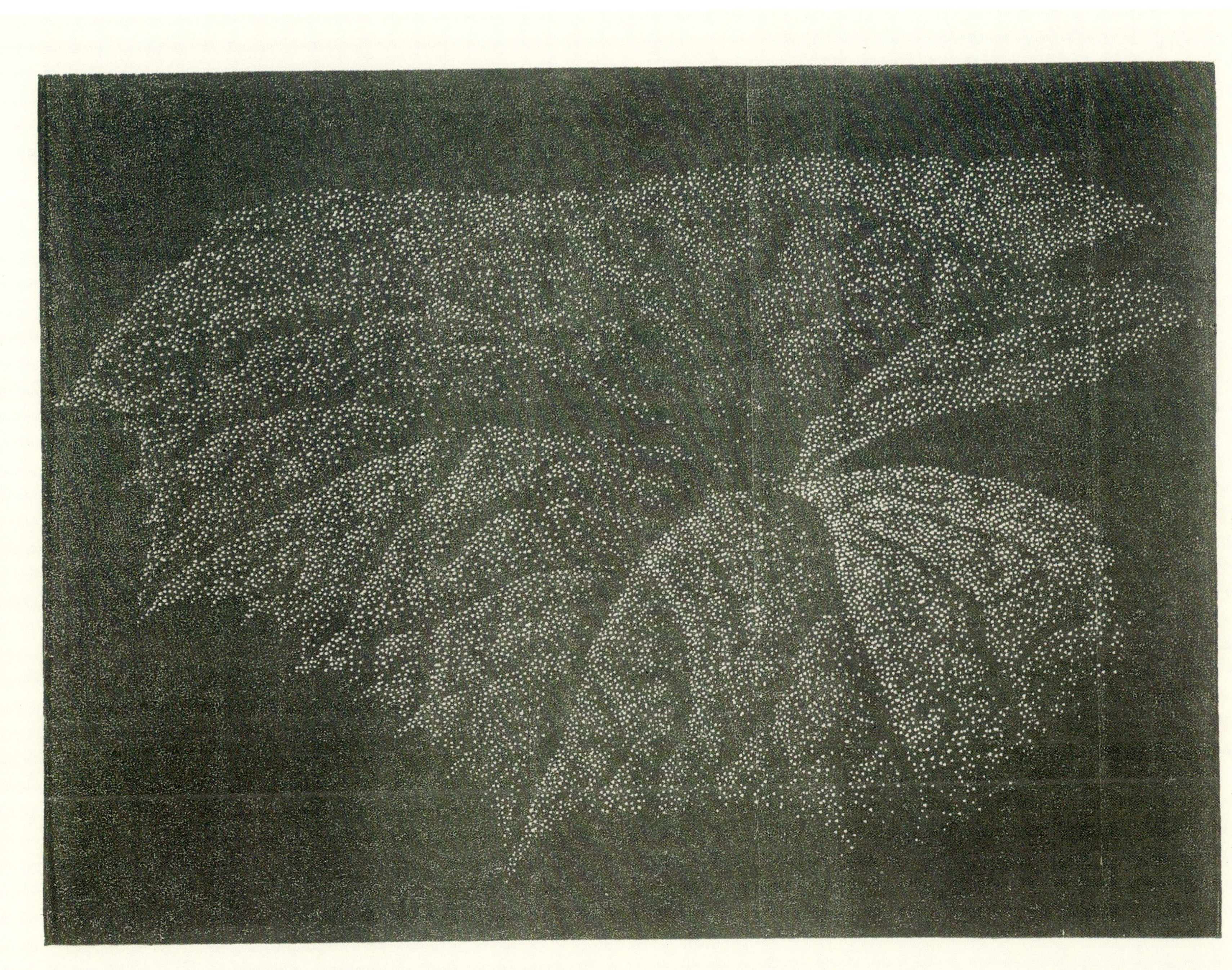

KATHY **GROVE**

In *The Other Series*, Kathy Grove reworks photographic reproductions of well-known works of art, eliminating the female figures. In *After Cézanne*, she removes the group of bathers from Paul Cézanne's *The Large Bathers* (in the collection of the Philadelphia Museum of Art), imitating the artist's brushstrokes to inpaint the space that remains. She performs the same reconstructive surgery on Eugène Delacroix's *Liberty Leading the People*, Masaccio's *Madonna Enthroned*, Henri Matisse's *Odalisque*, Man Ray's *Violin d'Ingres*, and André Kertész's *Satiric Dancer*, among some thirty other masterpieces. The mediums she uses vary from photogravures to gelatin silver prints to chromogenic prints to the silver dye bleach (Cibachrome) transparency and neon lightbox used for *After Cézanne*. This last has the added piquancy of reminding us of a slide projected for an art history exam, perhaps the ultimate reproduction and test of memory in the world of art.

The cumulative effect of *The Other Series* is one of surprise. It is as if the women pictured in all mediums throughout the history of art have come to life, acquired free will, and fled the scene, choosing not to participate in a posterity not of their own making. Their absence provokes conjecture: Who were they really and what do they represent? Why and how are they portrayed? They assume an existence in the mind apart from visceral line, form, and color. They become real women as well as figures in works of art.

Grove at first seems to fall within the postmodern trend of appropriation practiced by artists such as Sherrie Levine and Barbara Kruger. Her purpose, however, is not to challenge authorship or to confront cultural stereotypes but to redress the wrongs of history and reclaim works of art for today's society. MC

The Other Series: After Cézanne
1992
Silver dye bleach transparency in framed neon lightbox; edition of 3
21¼ x 24½" (54 x 62.2 cm) overall
1993-55-1

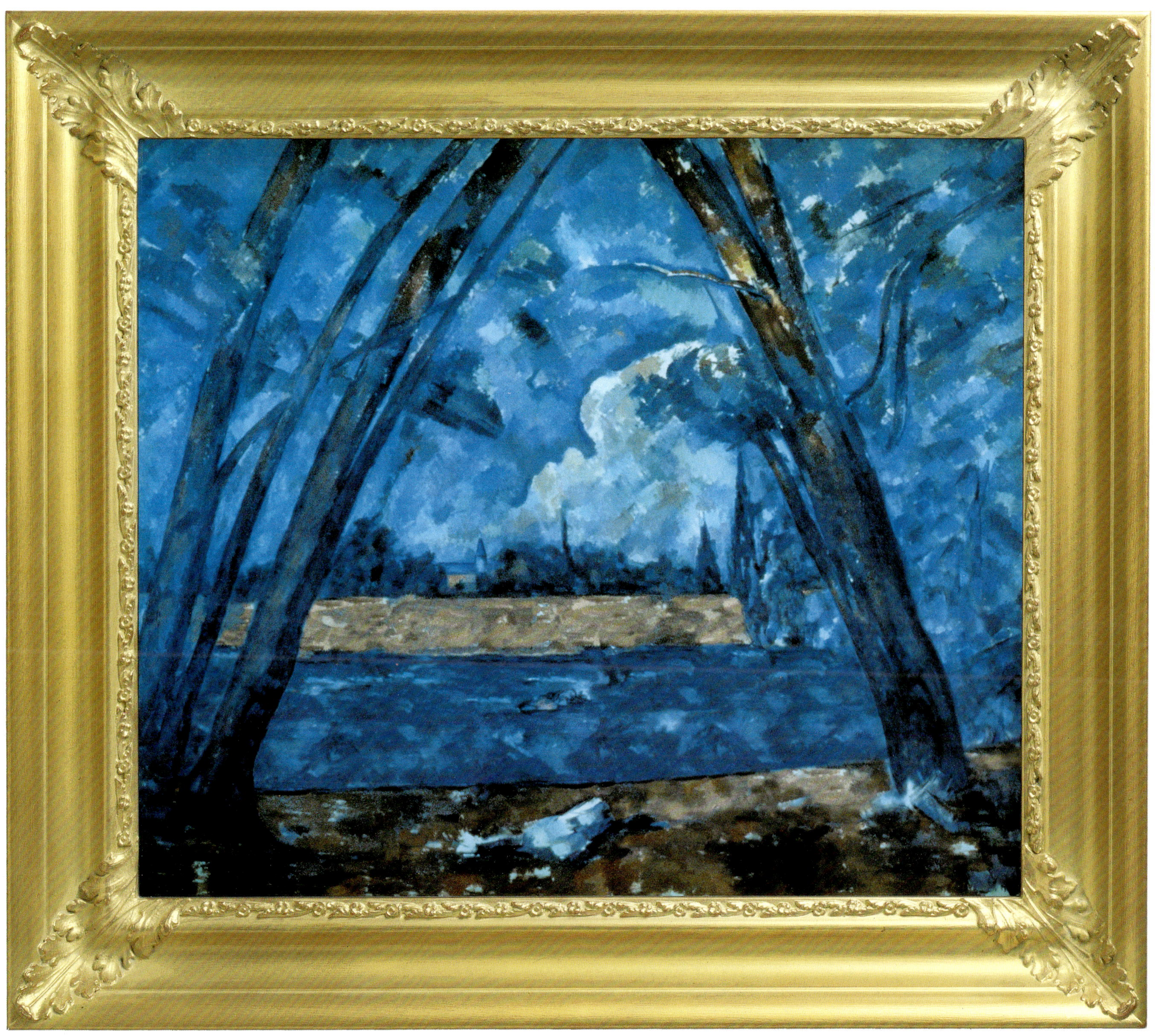

In Rick Hock's *Codex (Truth/Art)*, a grid of images from the history of art and popular culture forms an ideogrammatic diagram of a message in code. The grid is intuitive, nonhierarchical, and nonlinear. Investigation follows multidirectional pathways based on association, research, and contemplation. Unlike traditional photographs, Hock's codices nullify the expectation that either subject or meaning can be perceived directly. Hock tells us that to understand the world, we have to be prepared to make connections within a shifting vortex of ideas and images, many of which are hidden or crude or common or forgotten, and that any final interpretation we come to is ultimately reductive. Concurrently, Hock recognizes that among the strongest of human impulses is the need to make sense of things and to find a holistic world view.

Visual motifs from both high and low culture (note the proximity of an Arcimboldo painting and Wes Mess from Art Spiegelman's "Garbage Pail Kids") here suggest a connection between bodily appendages and coherence or integrity. Artificial hands and limbs, eyeballs, pipes, beards, canes, staffs, telephones, ties, masks, and the like proliferate in the context of art, making weird bedfellows of Marcel Duchamp, Norman Rockwell, Francis Bacon, Emmett Williams, Martin Schongauer, and Charles Willson Peale. Many other connections could be made through the work, such as the succession of bland, round faces. There is even a seemingly gratuitous, playful, audio pathway that joins the Dadaist Hugo Ball's phonetic poem "Karavane" to Jim Nutt's *Toot, Toot, Woo, Woo* to Santa Claus's "Ho Ho Ho" and perhaps to the phonetic fun of Luke Puke, Wes Mess, Ecce Homo, and the Laocoön. No routes through the codex are proscribed to the viewer. MC

RICK MCKEE **HOCK**

Codex (Truth/Art)
1988
Dye diffusion transfers on Arches watercolor paper
48¼ x 61" (122.6 x 154.9 cm) sheet
40¾ x 54" (103.5 x 137.2 cm) image
1989-38-1

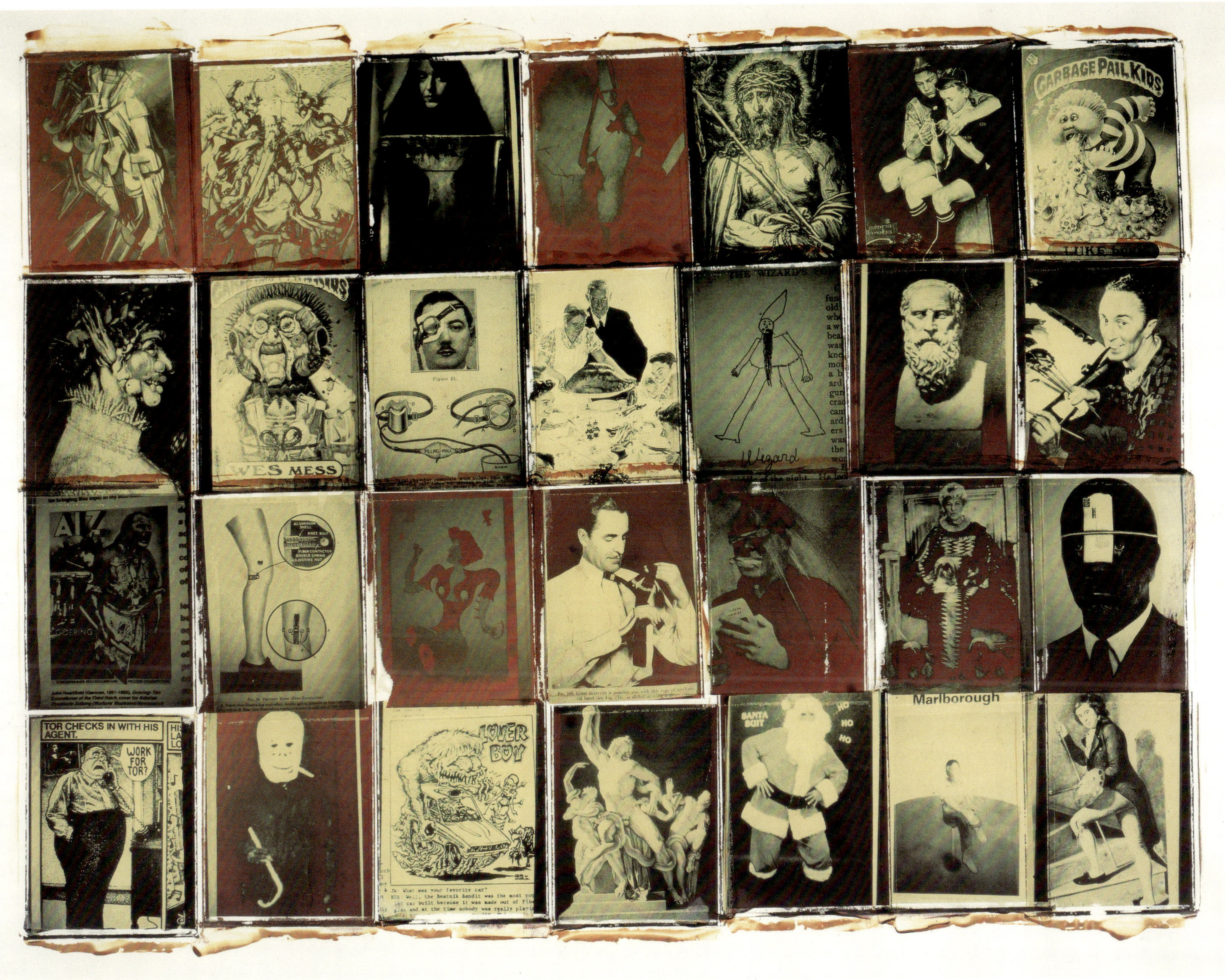
GARBAGE PAIL KIDS
WES MESS
Figure 21.
THE WIZARD'S
Wizard
AIZ
TOR CHECKS IN WITH HIS AGENT.
WORK FOR TOR?
LOVER BOY
SANTA SUIT
HO
HO
HO
Marlborough

Perhaps conceptual art can be, as in the case of Peter Hutchinson, the most personal kind. The ideas that give birth to Hutchinson's works of art spring from his experience as a traveler, student of nature, and gardener. Experiencing his works is to be drawn into the life of the artist, passing through gentle daydreams and unexpected associations, relishing tidbits of scientific fact offered up for wonderment and not the finality of definition, and glimpsing a mind on a fantastic voyage through a landscape made by time, nature, man, and artist.

Many works by Hutchinson made in recent years have been on the theme of the mixed landscape, where distant parts of the world are brought together in a way he suggests is like the cross breeding of plants or the introduction of exotic plants into non-native areas. The mixed landscape is a hybrid of places combined through mental and emotional associations, a metaphor for life as a composite of memories and experiences that form an internal reality.

Berlin-Mexico, as Hutchinson's text describes, is about the memory of a landscape encountered for the first time on a bus trip into Mexico, a memory that was awakened by a visit to the cactus house at the Berlin Botanical Garden, where arid desert conditions are recreated and desert plants are grown and labeled for study. Many years later, Hutchinson returned again to the cactus house and made the photographs for this work. He alludes to his two visits and two different experiences by repeating each image in the collage. Alterations in framing and the application of paint join the separate parts into a whole. MC

PETER **HUTCHINSON**

Berlin-Mexico
1988–89
Chromogenic color prints with applied gouache on rag board
40 x 50½" (101.6 x 128.3 cm)
1989-39-1

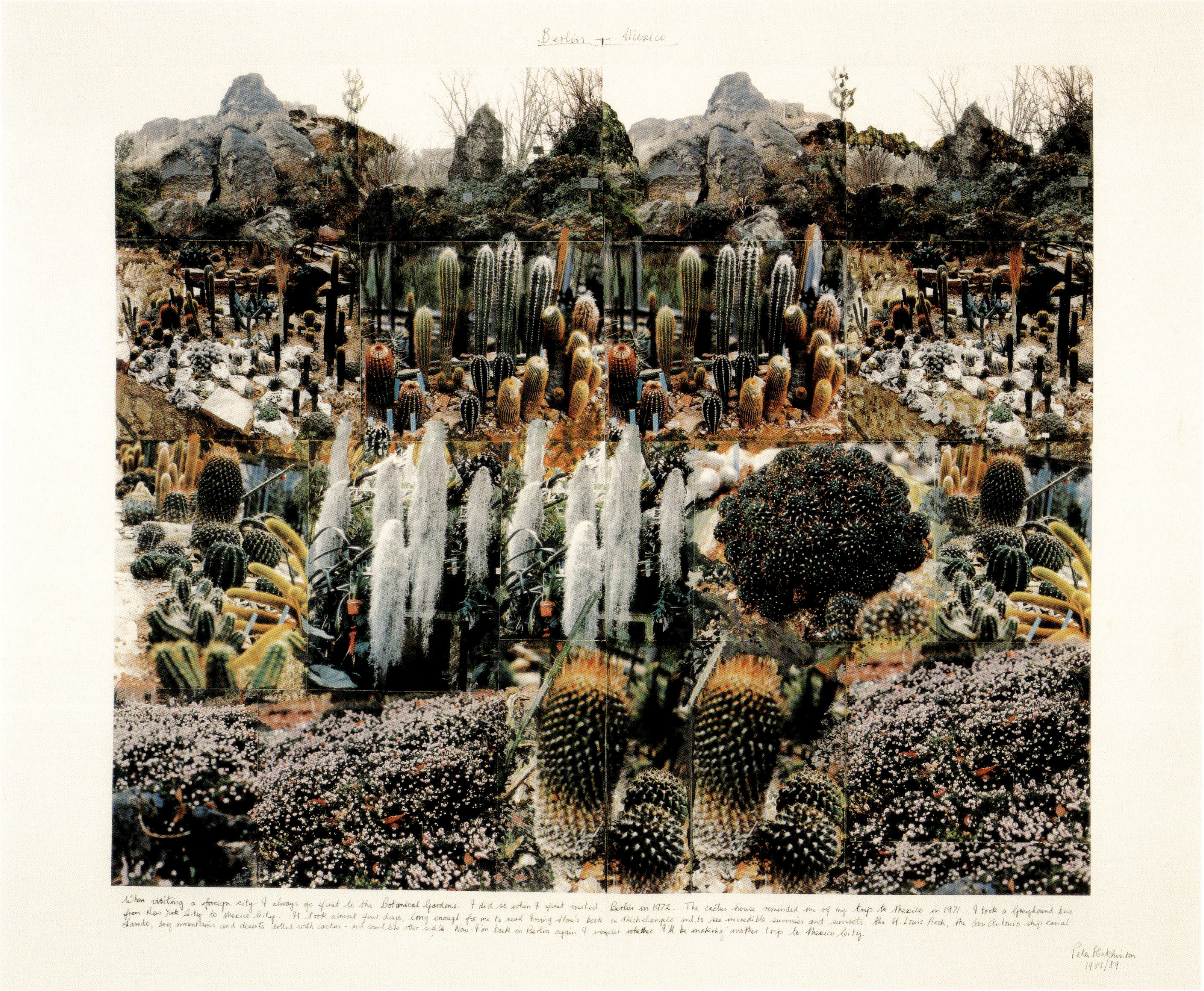

When visiting a foreign city I always go first to the Botanical Gardens. I did so when I first visited Berlin in 1972. The cactus house reminded me of my trip to Mexico in 1971. I took a Greyhound bus from New York City to Mexico City. It took almost four days, long enough for me to read Irving Stone's book on Michelangelo and to see incredible sunrises and sunsets. The St. Louis Arch, the San Antonio ship canal Laredo, dry mountains and deserts dotted with cactus – and countless other sights. Now I'm back in Berlin again I wonder whether I'll be making another trip to Mexico City.

Peter Hutchinson
1988/89

Anish Kapoor's works on paper incorporate a wide range of mediums, including gouache, gesso, charcoal, acrylic, powdered pigment, earth, ink, pencil, varnish, and papier-mâché. The images reflect not only the biomorphic or geometric shapes of his sculptures, but their coloration as well: intense primary colors together with browns, blacks, and whites. The drawings, however, are executed in a softer, more subtle way, with rich overlays of tones and frequent manipulations of the paper in curves and wrinkles, as if to incorporate its natural pliability into the image. Shapes are often attached to or built out from the surfaces of the papers, so that the line between drawing and three-dimensional object becomes blurred. Colors for Kapoor have specific associations: blue with the infinite, black or red with the earth, yellow with passion. His handling of paint involves a great deal of mysterious, often turbulent, splashing, brushing, layering, and texturing of colors. He creates shapes that suggest but do not actually represent natural phenomena such as plants, root systems, galaxies, human anatomy, or storms, in a way that is neither exactly organic nor abstract.

Kapoor is drawn to the concept of issues in binary opposition—solid and void, male and female, dark and light—which he sees as fundamental to an Indian view of the world. Commenting on one of his sculptures, he says:

It's a work about mass, about weight, about volume and then at the same time seems to be weightless, volumeless, ephemeral; it's really turning stone into sky. The darkness inside the stones is the darkness of black night, the darkness of sky. And it seemed that once I'd made "Void Field," this earth into sky object, it occurred to me that it would be wonderful to attempt the opposite. . . . Let's say in "Void Field" we have earth containing sky, earth outside, sky within. To do the opposite was to have earth within, sky without. I just painted some stones. And what they became . . . they became bits of sky.[1]

In his drawings, Kapoor seeks the same paradoxical denial of exactly defined subjects and categories. AP

1. Quoted in Constance Lewallen, "Interview with Anish Kapoor, Japan, September, 1990," *View*, vol. 7, no. 4 (Fall 1991), p. 21.

ANISH **KAPOOR**

Untitled
1988
Brown washes and graphite on toned paper
$21^{3}/_{4}$ x $20^{1}/_{2}$" (55.2 x 52.1 cm)
1989-40-1

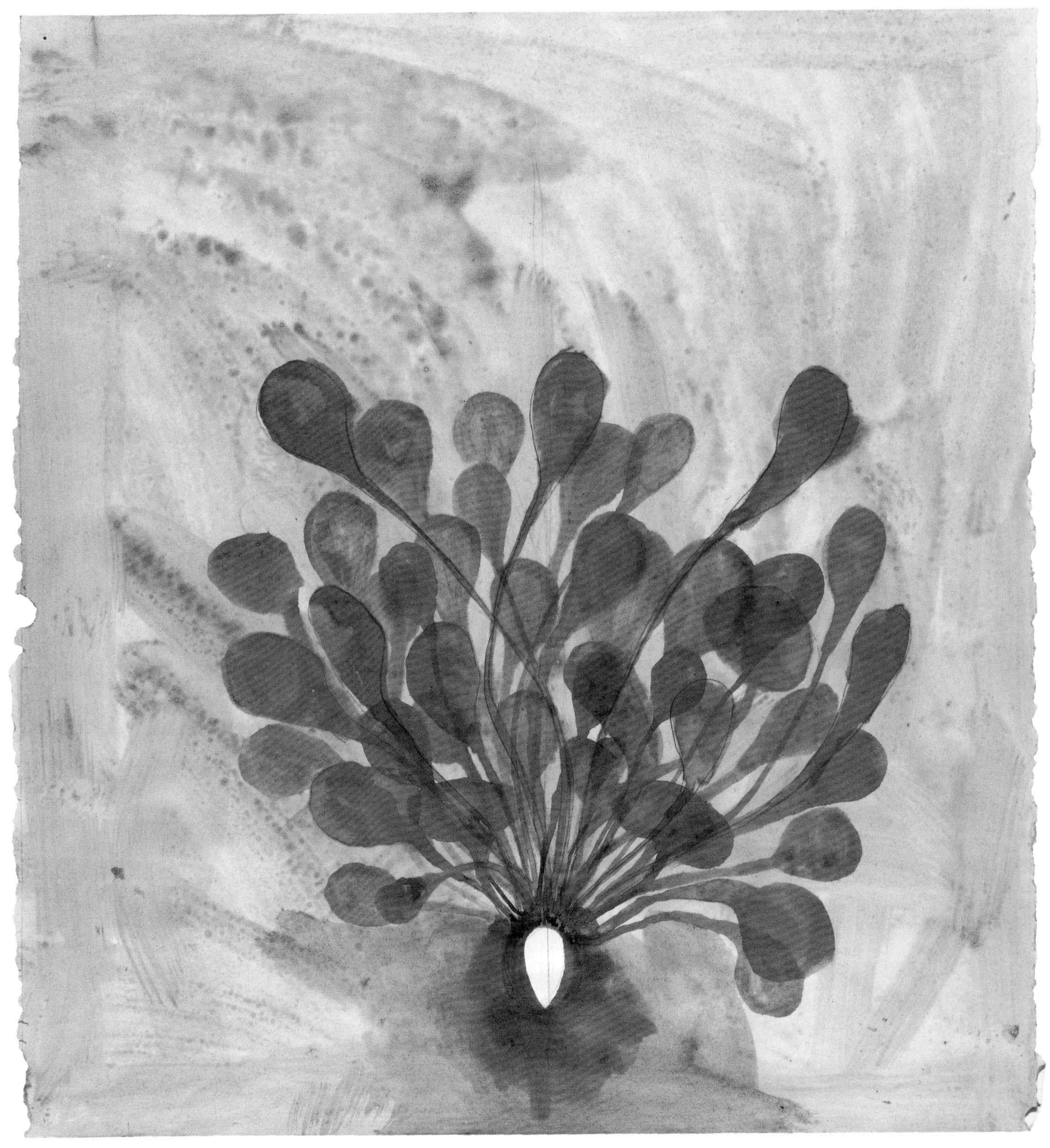

MEL **KENDRICK**

Although the enormous black-and-white works on paper that Mel Kendrick began to make in the early 1990s may at first seem to be a sharp departure from the wood sculptures for which he is best known, his works in both mediums actually share a number of physical characteristics. Both the sculptures and the drawings are comprised of large-scale, energetic shapes that seem as much organic as geometric or abstract in nature, and both emphasize the texture of wooden surfaces. Just as Kendrick's wood sculptures are composed of blocks of often exotic woods sawn apart and reassembled—incorporating angles, curves, twists, and tilts—the large drawings (or monoprints) are created from four-by-eight-foot sheets of plywood (both rough and more finished grades for contrasting textures), in some cases cut into abstract shapes with a bandsaw and assembled like jigsaw puzzles. The surface is then inked with printer's ink, over which Japanese paper is laid and rubbed with a bowl-shaped object, in a manner reminiscent of tomb or brass rubbings. The complex texturing from the wood grain, the austerity of the black ink and white paper, the monumental scale, and the existence of chance marks, such as screws, fingerprints, or nail heads, combine to make these works powerful and evocative statements about shapes, surfaces, textures, materials, craftsmanship, physical process, and object-making. In *Dovetail*, ink rubbings from two uncut sheets of rougher-grained plywood are visually joined by collaged "dovetail hinges" printed from plywood of a finer grain. Both the monoprints and the sculptures reaffirm the artist's preference for the sensuous, organic art object that evidences the handwork necessary for its creation. AP

Dovetail
1993
Relief monotype with collaged elements on two sheets of kozo paper mounted on canvas
108 x 96" (274.3 x 243.8 cm)
1993-123-1

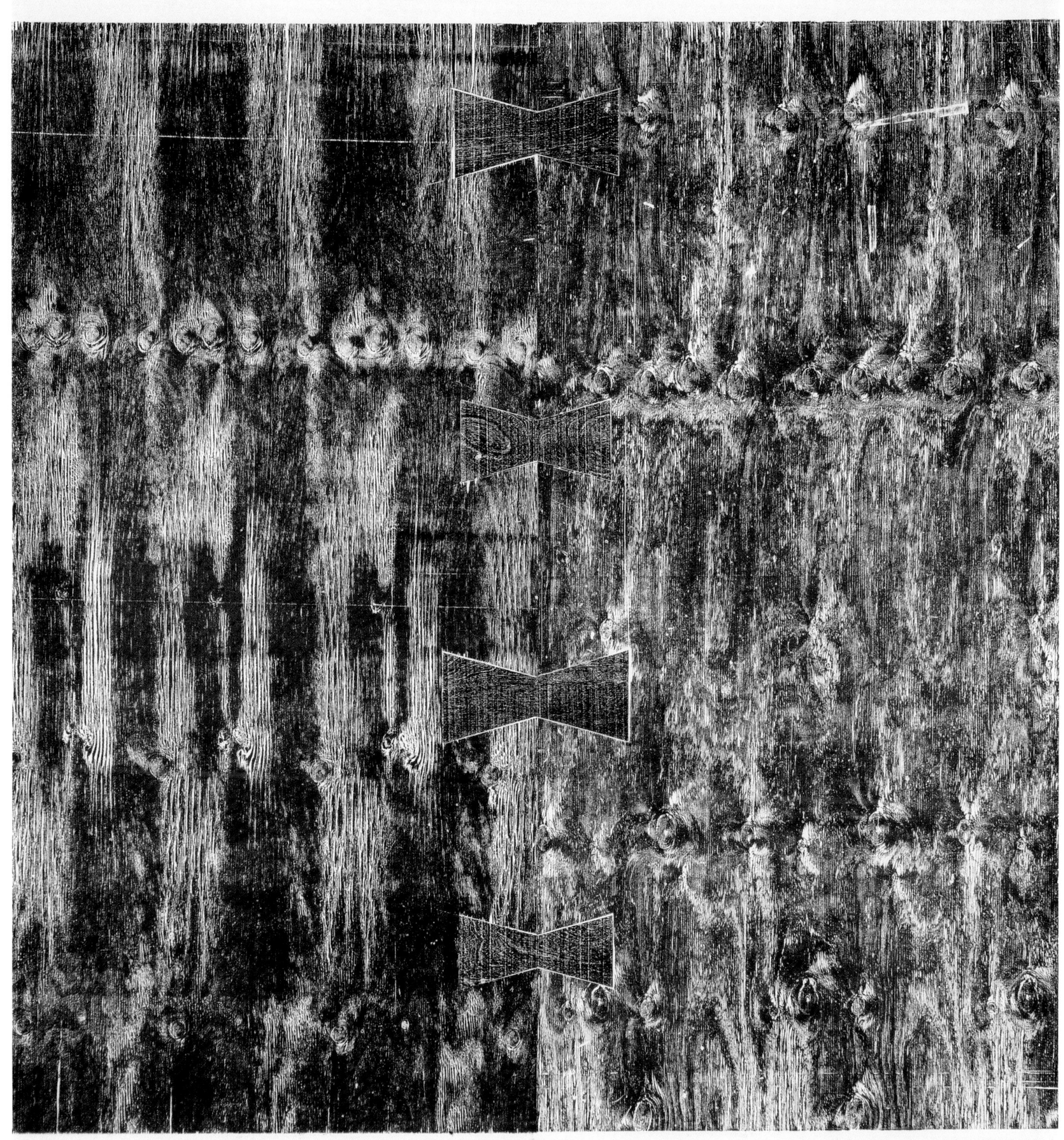

KOCOT AND **HATTON**

Marcia Kocot and Thomas Hatton's work tends to fall into various conceptual series of long evolution, such as the ten-year serial project of self-portraits that they undertook in 1973, which was intended to convey an ever-changing perception of their own identities. *Red, Yellow, and Blue* is part of an ongoing series entitled "8," which consists essentially of monotypes produced using inked bubble wrap instead of more traditional metal, stone, plastic, or glass plates. The "8" series was inspired by a 1987 announcement from the Kitt Peak Observatory of the discovery of three "mirage arcs" in star clusters on the perimeter of the universe, which the artists imagined to be "light reflecting back from the end of space."[1]

In the early 1990s, Kocot and Hatton began to suggest the idea of bounded infinity through ink drawings of traditional figure eights, which eternally return upon themselves, much like a Möbius strip. These ink drawings led to a series of works printed with ink on kraft paper using bubble wrap. These later works, for the most part, incorporate a digital representation of the number eight, a form inferring electronic space that reveals and obscures all numbers.

The patterns utilized in *Red, Yellow, and Blue*, derived from a nineteenth-century international color-code manual in which patterns symbolized colors, operate on a similar level, with a display of color that can be read so that it simultaneously presents color to the mind (the patterned codes) and to the eye (the pigments). The red pigment in the left panel of the triptych is reinforced by the vertical line pattern for red, whereas the green pigment in the central panel conforms to the chaotic pattern for yellow. In the right panel, the horizontal line pattern for blue amplifies the blue pigment.

Red, Yellow, and Blue presents additive (red, green, and blue) and subtractive (red, yellow, and blue) primary colors, using codes and pigments coexisting simultaneously. It is not a synthesis, but rather Kocot and Hatton's attempt to allow two concepts of color to occupy the same space at the same time. Paradoxes—such as the concept of dimensionless space, infinite yet bounded, or the symbolizing of one color through a pattern that is visually presented in another color—are fundamental to the artists' thinking. They force the viewer to confront new perceptions of self, of space, of scale, of perspective, and of the place of works of art in the viewer's consciousness. AP

1. Kocot and Hatton, artists' statement, August 30, 1990, n.p

Red, Yellow, and Blue,
from the "8" series
1993
AM Multigraphic ink printed from bubble-wrap plastic on three sheets of kraft paper
44 1/4 x 29 1/8" (112.4 x 74 cm) sheets
132 3/4 x 87 3/8" (337.2 x 221.9 cm) assembled
1993-57-1a,b,c

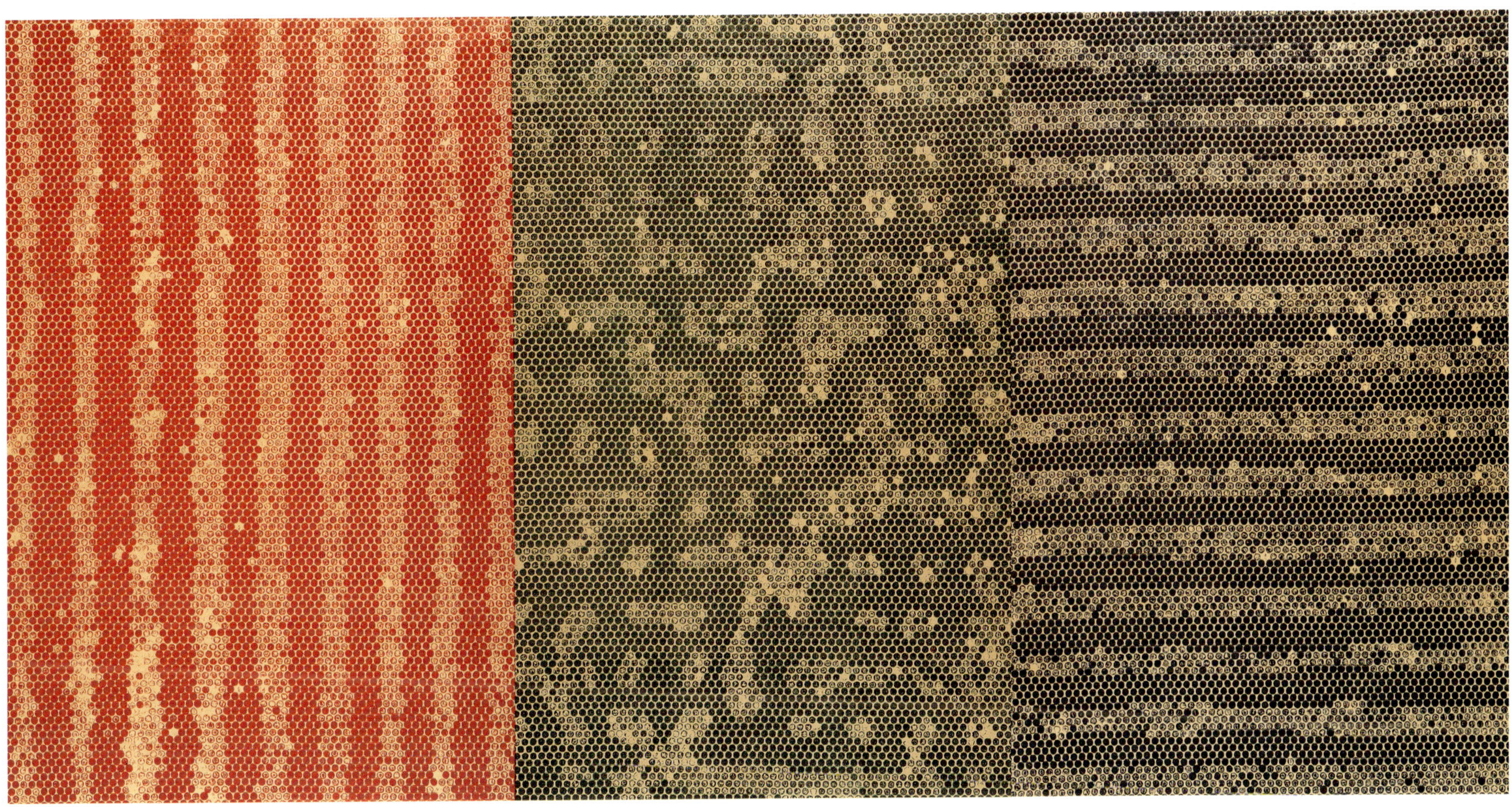

“The twelve-color woodblock prints in the portfolio ‘Meltdown’ have been created by Sherrie Levine by entering images, after Duchamp, Monet, Kirchner and Mondrian into a computer scanner that spatially quantizes and transforms these images into the minimum number of pixels, thus determining each of the colors in the four prints.”

Although the above text of the portfolio’s colophon does not provide a full explanation of the complex process involved in the production of *Meltdown*, it is absolutely indispensable for understanding the images. Distinguished more by the superior quality of printing and paper than by the force of the imagery, which consists of bland and pleasing juxtaposed squares of color, the woodblock prints are quite literally the “melted down” averages of the colors in each of four works: Marcel Duchamp’s *L.H.O.O.Q.*, a painting from Claude Monet’s *Rouen Cathedral* series, Ernst Ludwig Kirchner’s *Potsdam Square, Berlin*, and Piet Mondrian’s *Tableau No. II*. Interestingly, neither the titles of the prints nor the colophon specifically identifies the titles of these works—a fact no doubt attributable to Levine’s practice of creating distance between herself and the original work of art even as she uses it as the basis for creating a new work.

Rather than appropriating the imagery of the originals, as she had done in many of her earlier works, Levine transformed the originals for *Meltdown* into entirely different works of art through the use of the computer. She fed slides of the four originals taken from books into a program that reduced each work to twelve essential fields of color, which read as squares or “pixels.” She then provided color printouts to the printer, Maurice Sanchez, who matched the ink colors to them. Because the color of the white ink that was mixed with the colored inks changed significantly as it dried, many proofings of the colors were necessary to accurately match the computer printouts. To keep the colors from printing over one another on the edges, as might occur in lithography, Levine decided to make woodblock prints. The blocks were made by master woodworker Jim Cooper, who also fashioned a jig that fit them together in such a way that all twelve blocks could be printed in a single run.

Aesthetic qualities have always been important in Levine’s appropriations of other works of art, and the interplay of the technological with the subjective and the aesthetic is essential to the *Meltdown* portfolio. Here, for example, the sheer but textured Korean kozo paper enhances the grain of the printed woodblocks. Most surprising in these works are the unexpected results of the computer’s synthesis of the colors of the original works of art, as in the muted colors of *After Mondrian* and the limited range of *After Monet*. With characteristic humor and irony, Levine’s appropriations reach a new level of complexity in *Meltdown* through her technological reduction of historically famous works to bland, geometric color equivalents, and through her translation of these computer-generated images into woodcut, the oldest printing technique. IHS

SHERRIE **LEVINE**

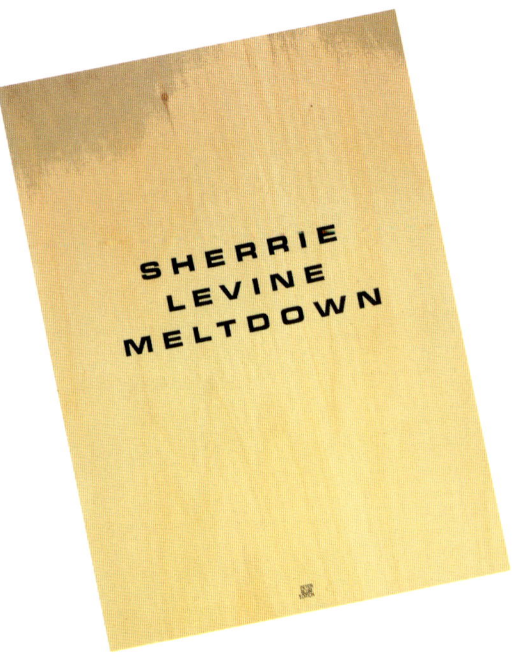

Meltdown: After Duchamp, After Monet, After Kirchner, After Mondrian
1989
Portfolio of four color woodcuts, each printed from twelve blocks on Korean kozo paper, in a case of poplar wood; edition 33/35; printed by Maurice Sanchez at Derrière l’Étoile Studios, New York; published by Peter Blum Edition, New York
24 x 18" (61 x 45.7 cm) images
36½ x 25¾" (92.7 x 65.4 cm) sheets
1990-13-1–4

Art reproductions used by Sherrie Levine to create the works in the *Meltdown* portfolio are (left to right): Marcel Duchamp, *L.H.O.O.Q.*; Claude Monet, *Rouen Cathedral, Façade*; Ernst Ludwig Kirchner, *Potsdam Square, Berlin*; and Piet Mondrian, *Tableau No. II*

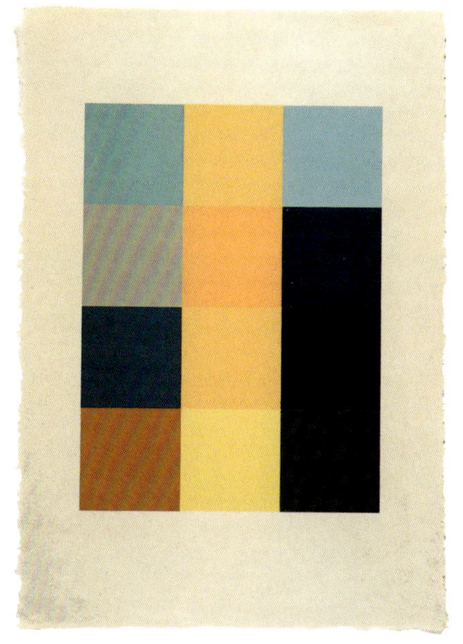

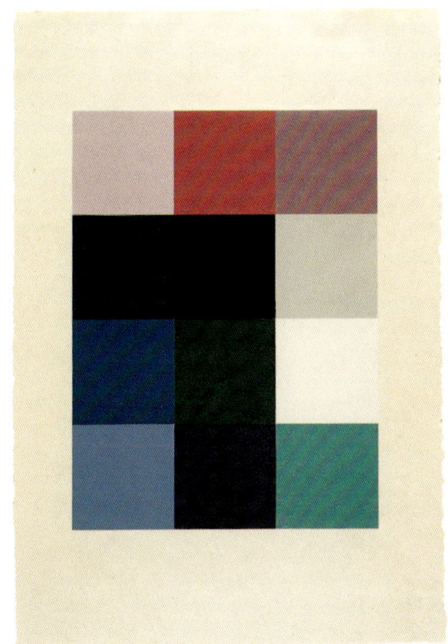

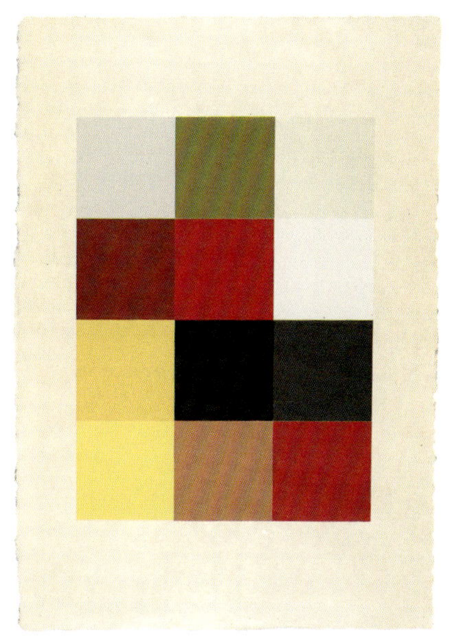

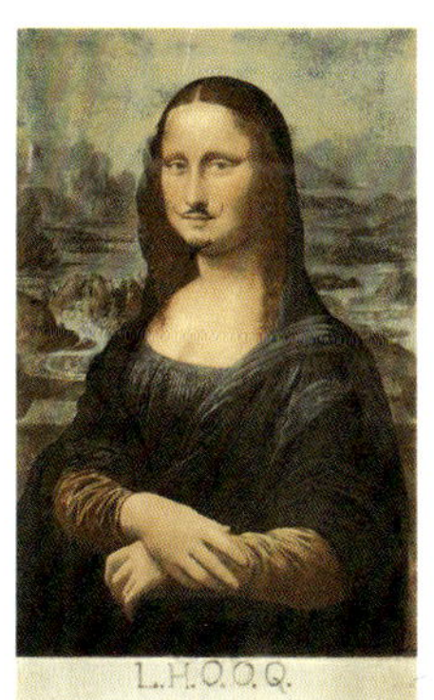
L.H.O.O.Q.

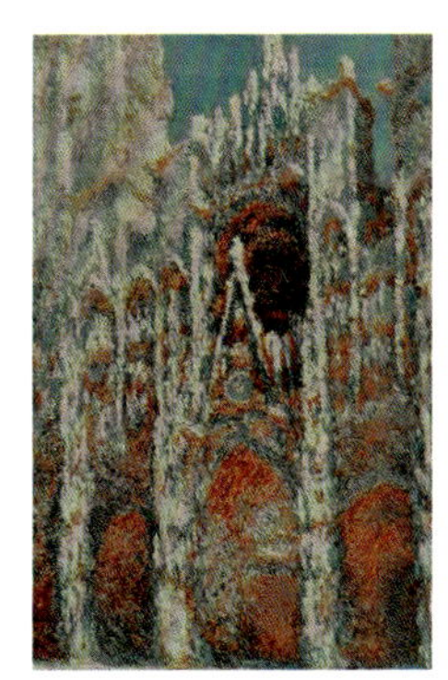

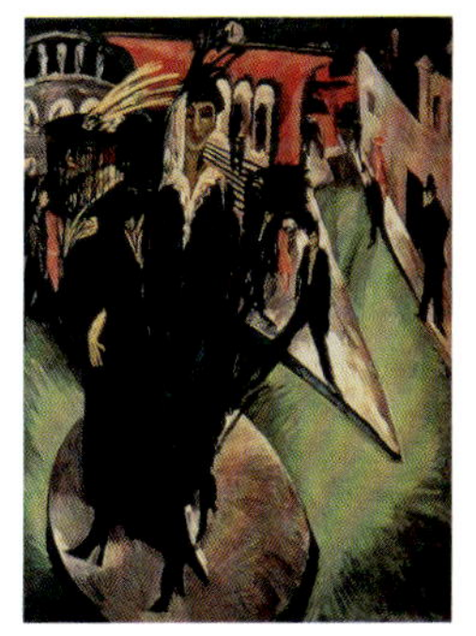

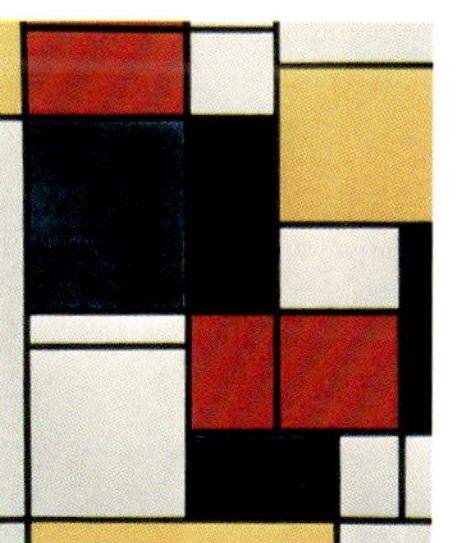

KATE **MORAN**

The physical manifestation of psychic injury in the female body is the melancholic subject of Kate Moran's photographs, objects, and installations. The body, its internal skeleton and organs, its external vestments, or its surrogates ache from violation and suffer from a sense of mortality and loss. Rarely is blame attached; the condition of being a woman simply brings with it a vulnerability to the mutilation of the psyche.

In the diptych *The Process of Making Dolls*, images of a female child and an androgynous doll are sewn together. The physicality of the stitching and the heavily waxed and incised surface of the two prints match the morbid intensity of the imagery. The object on the left side of the diptych resembles a child's coffin, although Moran's works are usually ambiguous and don't allow an easy or too-literal interpretation. A child's face floats up toward the surface like a memory. Multiple limbs are laid across the child's visage like exclamation points, amplifications of grief. Trauma is, by definition, repeated and relived in memory until it loses its grip.

On the right, a doll seems to shake its head in negation. Moran often uses dolls—which she constructs from clay, wax, and cloth—as works in themselves or in photographs. They appear in her work as fetish objects whose grotesquely unformed condition has a kind of inexorable and frightening reality. These dolls have hard, impenetrable surfaces, hollow interiors, and no distinguishable sex. They are more than surrogates for real children or women; because they participate in the psychic dramas of Moran's art but cannot be harmed, they might be seen as supernatural guardians. The "process of making dolls" can be seen as the process of making art, the healing and transcendent process that can exorcise pain. MC

The Process of Making Dolls
1994
Two gelatin silver prints with applied color, wax, and thread
48 x 62½" (121.9 x 158.8 cm)
1994-179-1

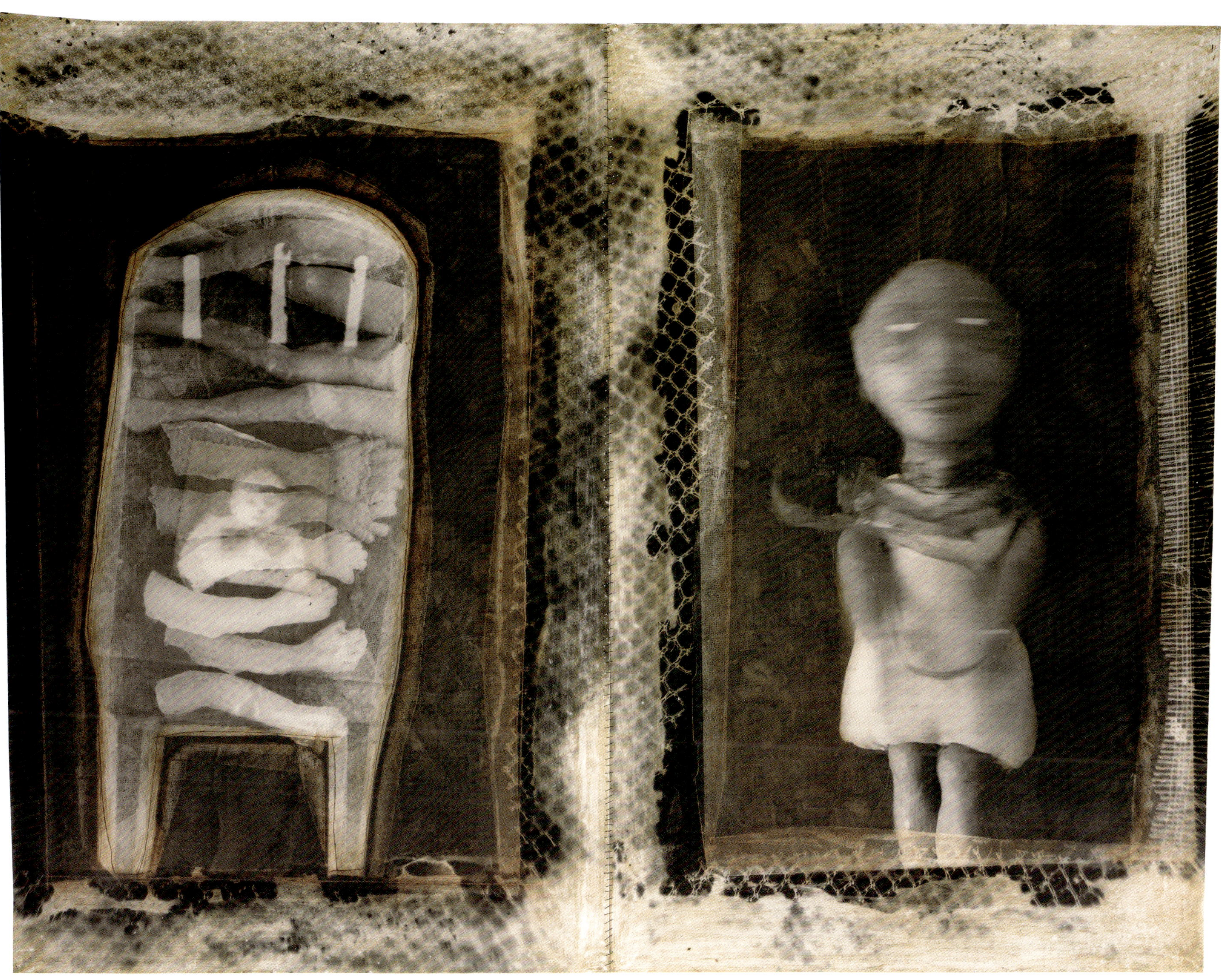

Among contemporary artists who appropriate ideas and images from "low" sources such as comic books or pulp fiction, Raymond Pettibon is admired for the singularity of his vision and the integrity of his artistic production. His oeuvre consists almost entirely of smallish ink and wash drawings with accompanying handwritten or handprinted texts. His method of working is cumulative, both in its process and in its presentation. His visual images and their concomitant texts—which take the form of musings, pronouncements, admonitions, or fragmentary sentences and phrases—are culled from a wide range of sources, such as books, magazines, movies, and television. In a typical installation, quantities of his drawings are casually pinned around the walls of a gallery and stacked or scattered on its floor. Because Pettibon works with multiple images that gain power when seen in numbers, four sheets are shown here. These demonstrate the variety of sentiments that the artist's drawings evoke, from the enigmatic to the sardonic, and from the elegiac to the absurd.

Pettibon's drawings provide constant surprise. Images derived from comic books and rendered in a straightforward, matter-of-fact graphic style are combined with texts that range from polished, elegant, occasionally arcane quotations—incomplete, out of context, and perhaps altered—to gritty and profane dialogue. The apparently casual juxtapositions are in fact the result of a subtle and deftly visualized relationship between word and picture. The works come across variously as witty, violent, moralizing, hallucinogenic, cruel, poetic, sadistic, or lyrical, although the shock of the sordid or salacious, as well as the high seriousness of the more literary quotations, is tempered by the mundanity of the images. Certain signature motifs, such as surfers, trains, and baseball players, recur in these drawings, whose themes range from sexual innuendo and a sort of defused violence to quasi-religious and philosophical allusions—both the sublime and the squalid sides of life being evoked with equal obsessive intensity. AP

RAYMOND **PETTIBON**

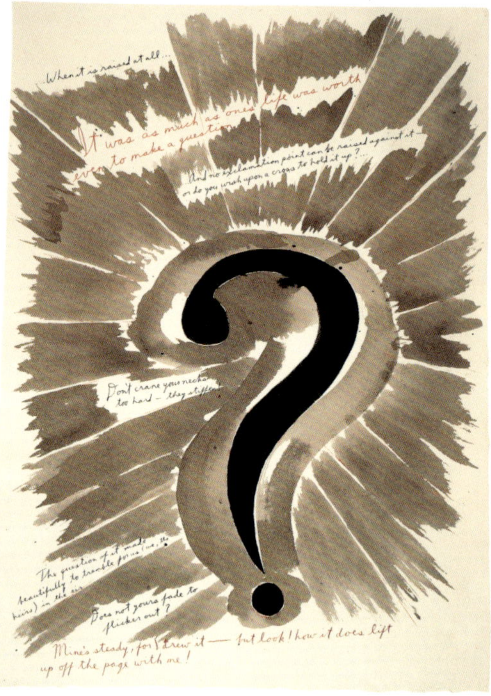

Untitled (When It Is Raised at All)
1992
Pen, brush, and ink on paper
$22^1/_8$ x $16^3/_8$" (56.2 x 41.6 cm)
1995-44-2

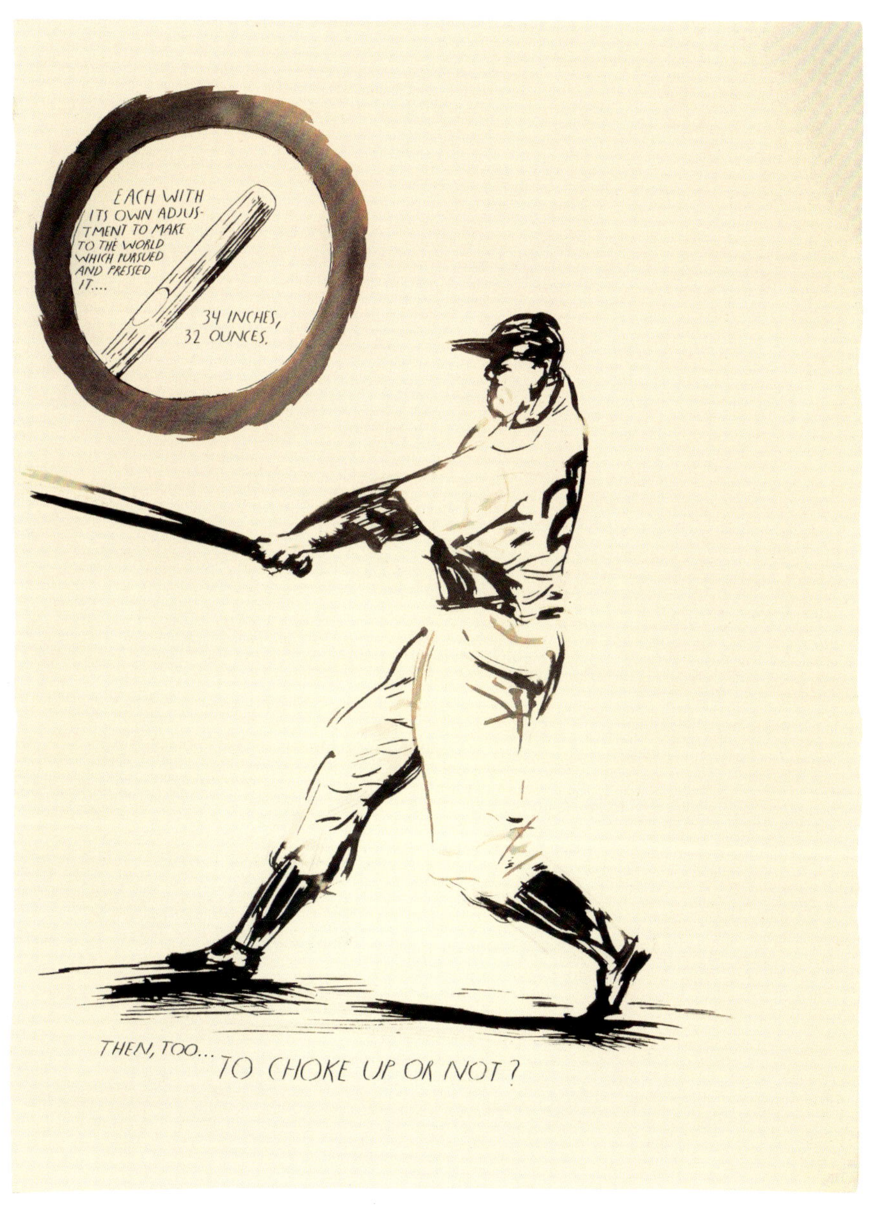

Untitled (Each with Its Own Adjustment)
1992
Pen, brush, and ink on paper
29⅞ x 22⅛" (75.9 x 56.2 cm)
1995-44-1

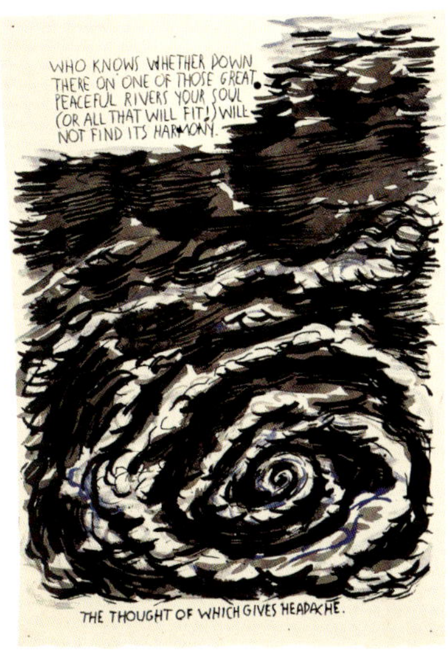

Untitled (Who Knows Whether)
1992
Pen, brush, and ink on paper
11 x 8" (27.9 x 20.3 cm)
1995-44-3

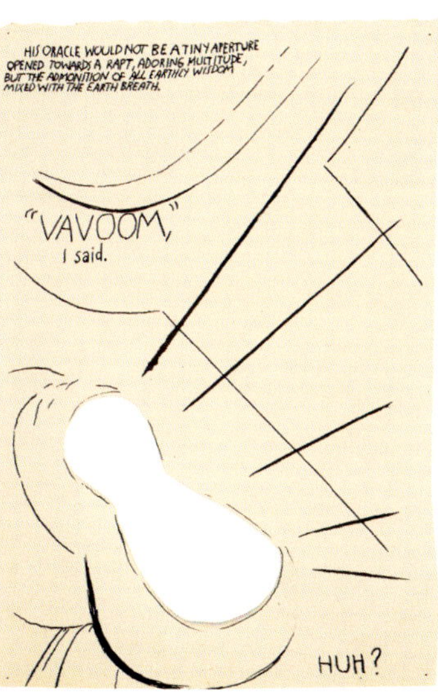

Untitled (His Oracle Would)
1993
Pen and ink on paper
10⅜ x 7⅛" (26.4 x 18.1 cm)
1995-44-4

JUDY **PFAFF**

The large-scale collage drawings on which Judy Pfaff has concentrated in recent years, although fundamentally two-dimensional, exhibit the same spatial ambiguities, complex combinations of disparate materials, and drastic shifts in scale that characterize the room-sized multimedia installations, or "environments," for which she is best known. The environments—created from many kinds of materials, such as plastic, wire, metal tubing, and found objects, usually brightly colored—are exuberant, often almost jarring; in them a high-pitched, frenzied energy seems reined in just at the edge of chaos. The drawings are mellower and subtler, but they display similar concerns with the tensions between the natural or organic object and the slick production of modern technology, and with the complexity of fluidly defined, intersecting layers of space in which no single viewpoint dominates.

An impression of flux prevails throughout *Mandrake*: images of flowers or plants merge into those of butterfly wings or animal skeleton fragments; veils of wax partially obscure whole areas, and a thick wash of transparent acrylic resin irregularly encases large portions of the surface. Scorches and burns curl the edges of the paper, which is ambivalently layered, torn, cut, and pieced; holes and tears punctuate its wrinkled and irregular surfaces. Few continuous edges are allowed to occur, making it hard to see where most parts of the work begin and end and impossible to judge how many elements are layered one over the other, where one stops and another starts. Scale shifts dramatically from small details of plants and flowers cut from botanical illustrations to broad splotches of bright red, green, or yellow paint and deep earth browns. There is an elemental quality—suggestive of earth, air, fire, and water—to the choice of materials and processes, in the images of flowers, plants, and insect wings, and in the scorches, tears, and burns, combined with layers of clear transparent material. In the upper right section of the work appears the image that gives it its title, a mandrake plant, which was once thought to have magical powers because its forked root resembles the lower half of the human body. A P

Mandrake
1994
Photocopy transfer, collaged botanical prints, wax, acrylic resin, oil stick, burns, graphite, and watercolor on Hosho paper
84 x 55" (213.4 x 139.7 cm)
1995-11-1

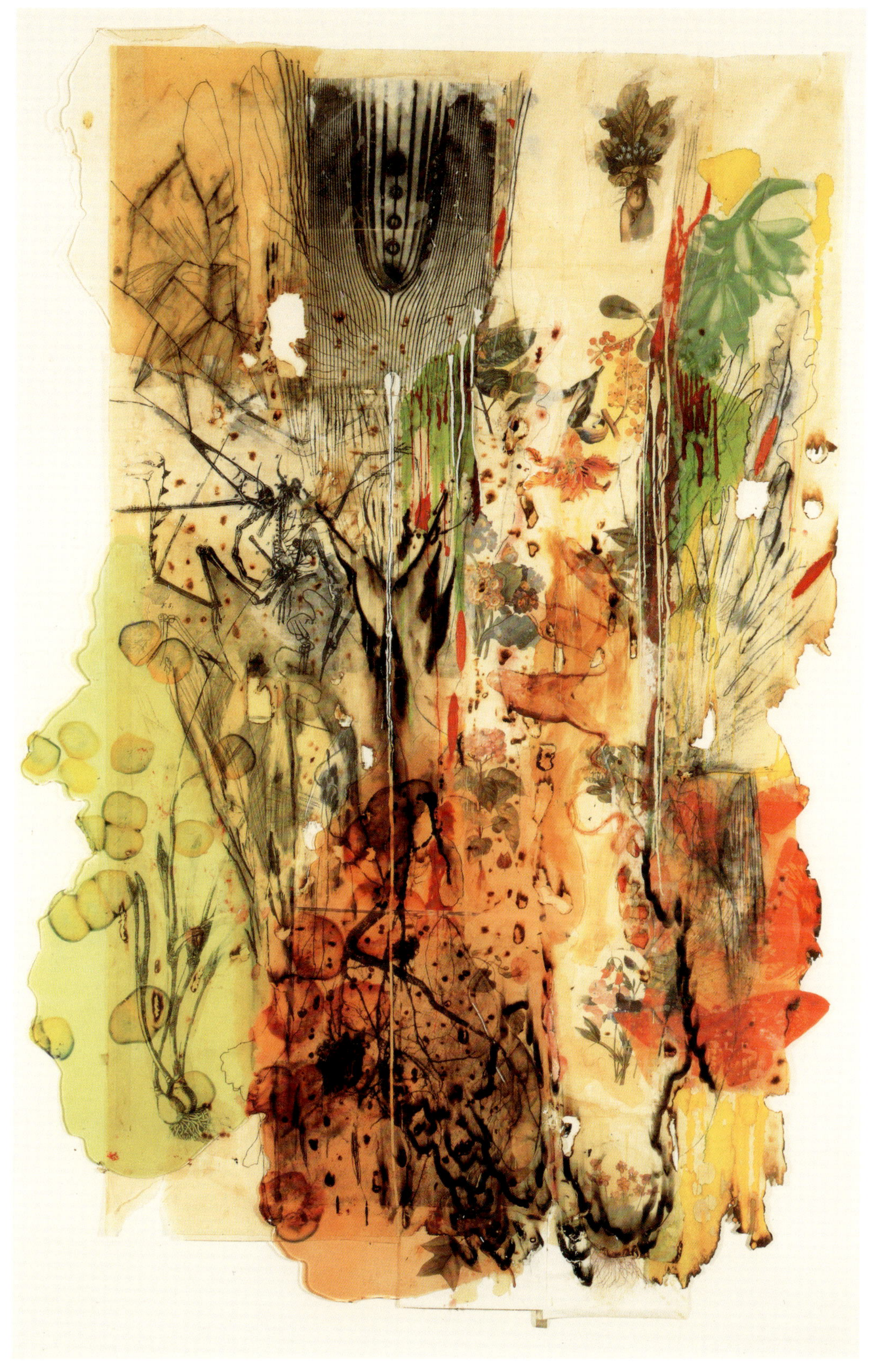

In his continual investigations of the interactions between vision and perception, language and meaning, Markus Raetz conjures punning and playful imagery out of an endless variety of carefully staged visual effects. In one work, a handful of dried eucalyptus leaves arranged on a wall traces the outline of a face; in another, a sheet of metal is bent in such a way that, when viewed from one angle, it appears as the profile of Joseph Beuys, the German artist-magus of the twentieth century, while from another it becomes the silhouette of a rabbit—the quintessential Beuysian emblem.

A magician of line, Raetz here combines commonplace materials—wire and paper—with the insubstantial elements of photography—light and shadow—to capture an evanescent subject—smoke wafting from the bowl of a pipe. As if in a sequence of stop-action frames recording the evolution of one of his optical illusions, Raetz here teases the viewer with deft sleight of hand. An oddly bent wire is first dangled in the light to fix its shadow on photo-sensitive paper—the closer the wire to the paper, the darker and crisper the line. In each of six stacked plates, the wire is turned and the shadow transformed until, in a final twist, the outline snaps into the shape of a pipe, à la René Magritte, out of which rise five amorphous puffs of smoke. JI

MARKUS **RAETZ**

Schatten (Shadows)
1991
Color photogram, photogravure, and aquatint printed from six plates and two larger background plates on Somerset cold-pressed (textured) paper; edition 25/35; printed (by Lothar Osterburg with the assistance of Pamela Paulson) and published by Crown Point Press, San Francisco
54½ x 12¼" (138.4 x 31.1 cm) image
69½ x 26½" (176.5 x 67.3 cm) sheet
1992-139-1

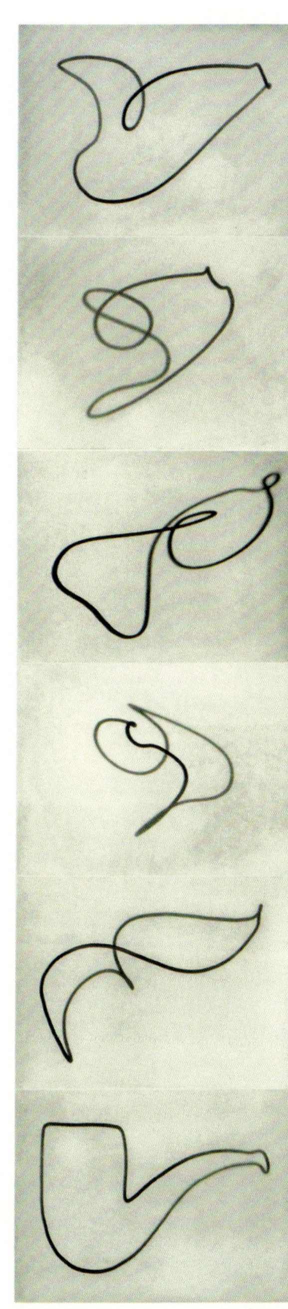

GERHARD **RICHTER**

Gerhard Richter has had one of the most diverse and elusive careers of the late twentieth century, primarily because of his use of photography. Describing his initial attraction to photography, he has stated that "there was no style, no composition, no judgement. It liberated me from personal experience. There was nothing but a pure picture. Therefore, I wanted to possess it and show it—not to use it as a means for painting, but to use painting as a means for the photograph."[1] Virtually all of his work since 1962 has been rooted in the photograph as a model.

Richter's use of the photograph as the source for his paintings has generated much critical speculation because it obscures the artist's relation to the conundrums of objectivity versus subjectivity, detachment versus emotion, representation versus abstraction, and mechanization versus manipulation. Richter does not employ the photograph in order to transform it or merely to copy it. Within his work, the photograph and the painting have equal validity, while at the same time in various ways, both are negated with equanimity.

In *5. Juli 94 (July 5, 1994)*, Richter uses the photograph itself as the support for his impastoed oil paint, applied in the manner of his abstract painting. The photograph, one he took on his travels, is just a photograph, with no compositional strength or intrinsic beauty. The paint is exultant, full of life and feeling, yet the presence of the photograph persists. There is no clue to the relationship between the photograph and the paint. The work could be interpreted literally as a picture of a house in flames. But since Richter neither affirms nor denies literal interpretation, it could just as easily have nothing to do with this interpretation.

Many critics see in Richter's work an indefinable quality that may have something to do with the state of the world at the end of the century. It is as if Richter, acting from a hypothesis that current methodologies and human consciousness do not contain the catalysts to evolution, chooses to posit a cultural ground of plurality, tolerance, equality, and openness. MC

1. Quoted in Rolf Schön, "Unser Mann in Venedig," *Deutsche Zeitung*, April 14, 1972, p. 13; reprinted and translated in *Gerhard Richter: 36. Biennale di Venezia* (Essen: Museum Folkwang, 1972), p. 23.

5. Juli 94 (July 5, 1994)
1994
Chromogenic color print with applied oil paint
4 x 6" (10.2 x 15.2 cm)
1995-43-1

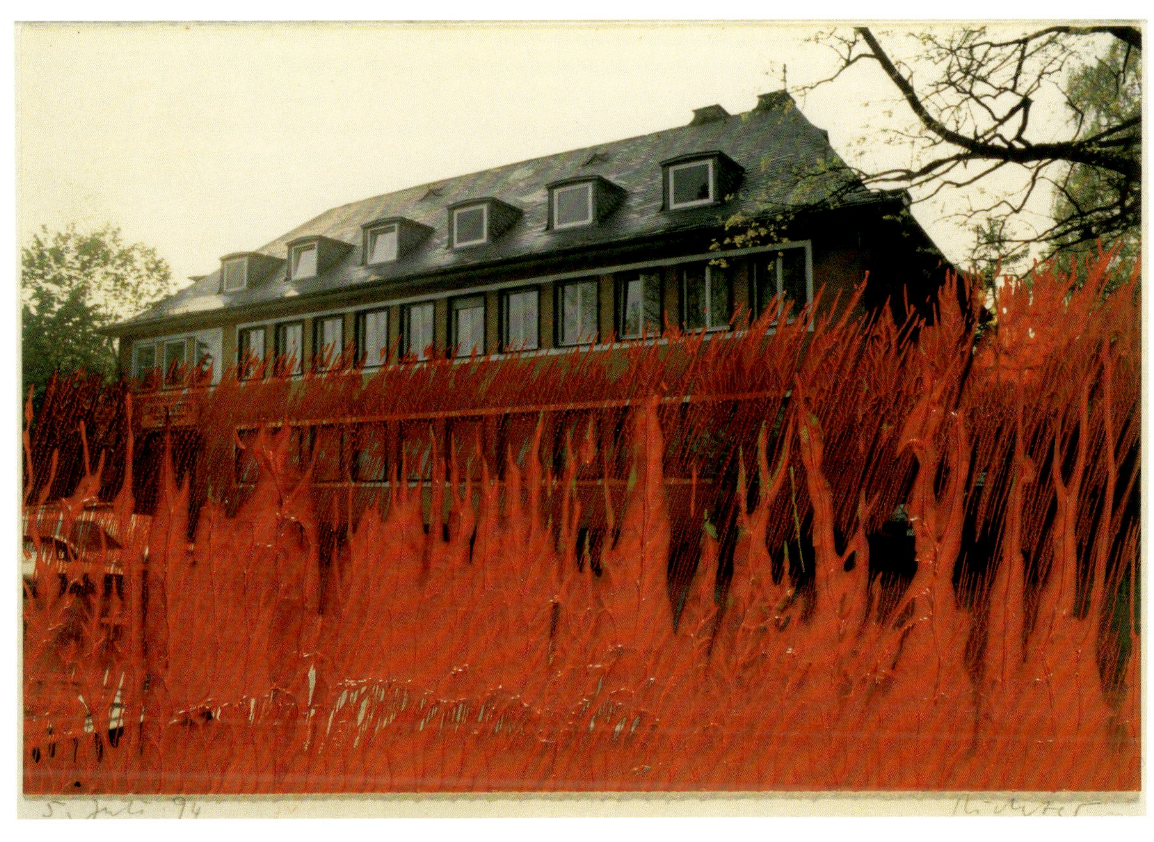

EDWARD **RUSCHA**

Ed Ruscha's facility in making art with unconventional materials—in the early 1970s he concocted his own pigments for paintings and prints out of a variety of food stuffs—allowed him to tackle the Mixografia printmaking technique employed in *Dog* with customary ingenuity. Working with a drawing on Mylar, the artist burnished the profile of the dog into the surface of a wax matrix and stippled the soft background, then impressed the foreground with an armful of tall grass cut from his own fields. The copper plate cast from the wax model was then inked: recesses left by the grasses were swabbed by hand in lifelike green, ocher, and yellow, while the dog and the stippled background were rolled with black ink.

With a visual vocabulary rooted in the commercial imagery of twentieth-century popular culture, Ruscha records the dreams and memories of everyday America. Although he first gained a reputation for his strange combinations of typography and text floating on lush-colored backgrounds, in the mid-1980s, while working on a mural commission for a library in Florida, he began a series of dark, soft-edged pictures drained of color and wordplay. These evocative, shadowy images inspired Ruscha to produce a group of silhouetted shapes executed later as paintings or prints, including *Dog*. Like many of the other ghostlike subjects Ruscha created during the 1980s, *Dog* is a solitary image stripped down to the emblematic spareness of a trademark or icon, with the haunting power to tap into our feelings of comfort and fear, loneliness and desire. JI

Dog
1994
Color Mixografia on handmade paper; edition 31/75; printed (by Isaias Remba and Wbaldo Muñoz) and published by Remba Gallery/Mixografia Workshop. West Hollywood
$27^{1}/_{4}$ x $38^{5}/_{8}$" (69.2 x 98.1 cm)
1994-180-1

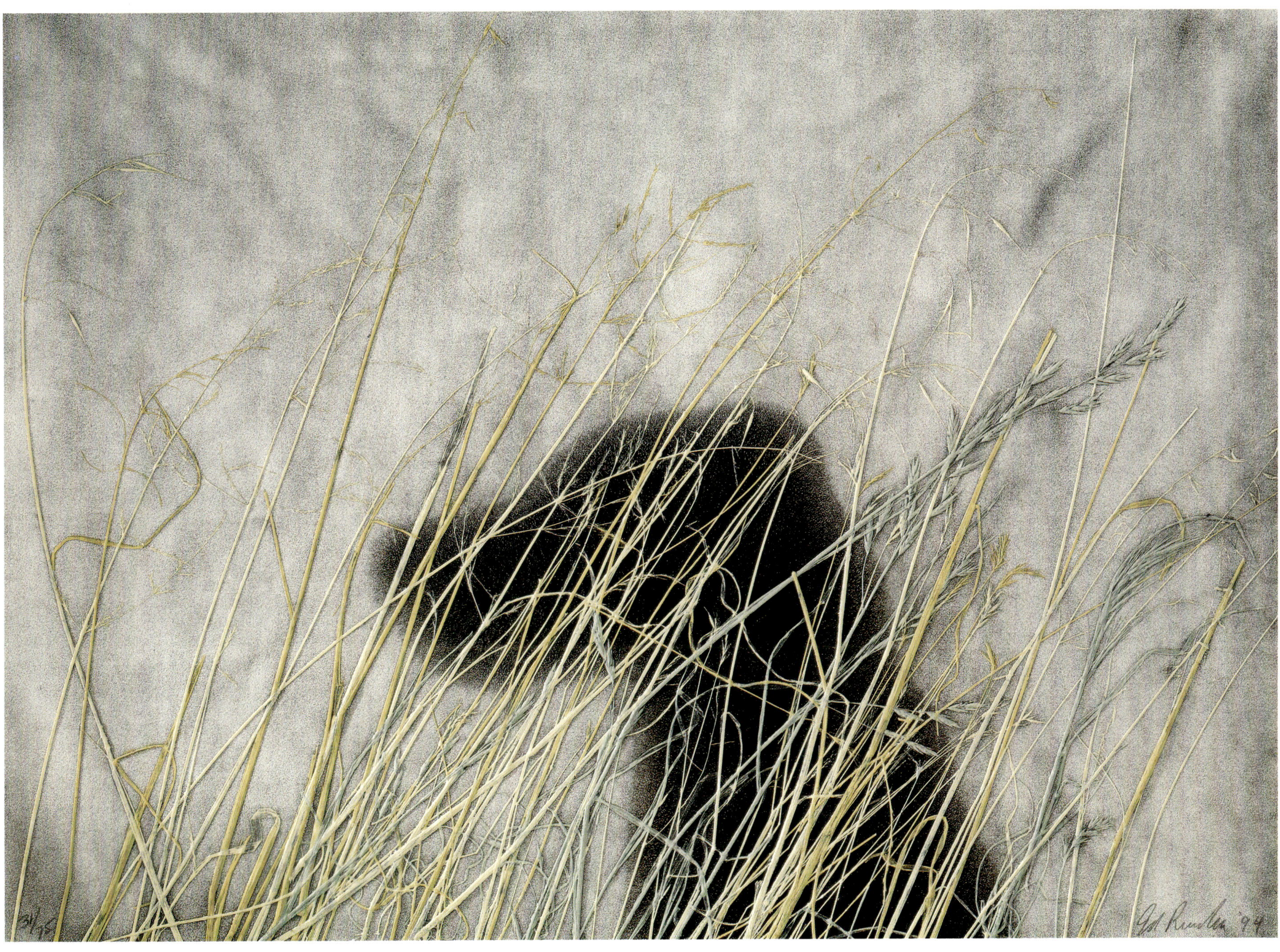

ALISON **SAAR**

A woman of Northern European, African American, and Native American ancestry who has made a close study of new-world African culture, Alison Saar freely interweaves strands of her own mixed racial heritage with Haitian voodoo, Cuban *santería*, and other rites. In *Blue Plate Special*, the brutal image of a severed head on a platter packs the punch of the gripping depictions by African American artists of Southern lynchings in the 1930s, while the gruesome visual pun contained within the title gives a surprising "pop" spin to a centuries-old tale from the Bible. Saar here depicts a black John the Baptist, an interpretation first effected by the artist in 1988 in a life-size figure of Salome about to kiss the lips of the decapitated saint. Saar regards Salome as a woman swept away by passion, with "the wrong kind of infatuation with the wrong guy,"[1] and in her work she casts Salome and John in roles of doomed black lovers, akin to "Frankie and Johnny" in the popular American folk ballad. The backdrop and frame, furnished by the decorative pattern of a pressed-tin ceiling square (one of Saar's favorite junkyard finds), call to mind the humble paraphernalia of homemade Southern folk reliquaries invested with spellbinding power. JI

1. Quoted in Judith Wilson, "Hexes, Totems and Necessary Saints: A Conversation with Alison Saar," *Real Life*, vol. 19 (Winter 1989), p. 40.

Blue Plate Special
1993
Color transfer lithograph, soft-ground etching, and *chine collé* on Arches cover paper; edition 16/20; printed (by Randy Hemminghaus and Jonathan Higgins) and published by Vinalhaven Press, Vinalhaven, Maine
24 1/8 x 24 1/2" (61.3 x 62.2 cm) image
28 3/4 x 28 3/4" (73 x 73 cm) sheet
1994-62-1

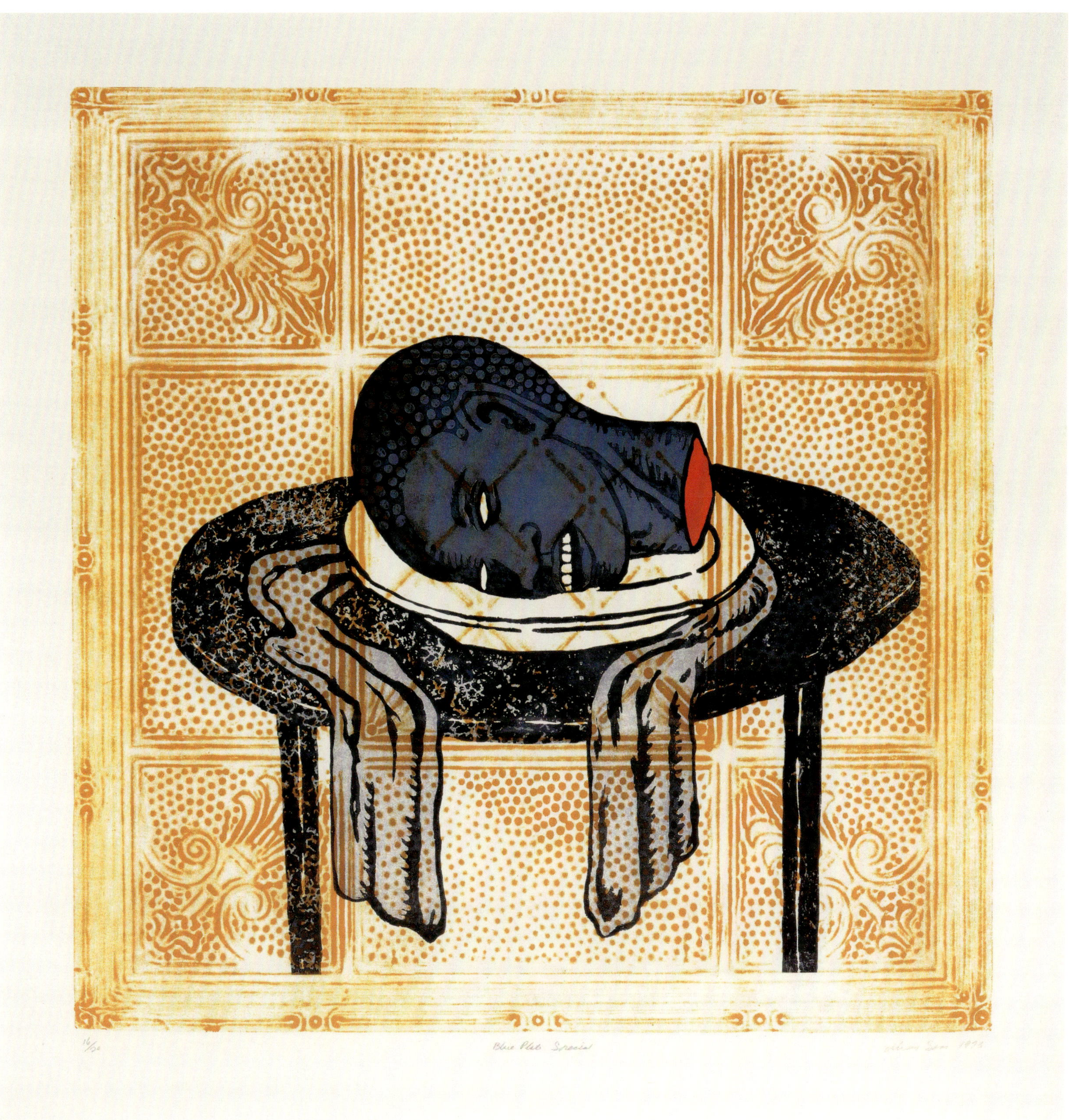

Dubbed "The Hair Print" at the time of its execution, Kiki Smith's untitled lithograph is printed sequentially in layers from nine lithographic stones and one plate. Altered by scraping and scratching, each stone bears the delicate tracery of the artist's own hair, transferred from photocopies and amplified by the incorporation of a full-length "Cher Hair" wig. Three corners of the sheet bear the cadaverous imprint of a rubber cast of the artist's head, split and splayed to show the right and left sides of her face (upper right and left) and the back of her neck (lower right), as if to fulfill Smith's stated desire to "unfold the human body." Unschooled in drawing, the artist here uses strands of hair graphically, creating a hypnotic interlace of swirling lines that serves as an organic metaphor for cross-hatching, a fundamental principle of academic draftsmanship.

For more than a decade, Smith has been a leading figure in a generation of artists who use the human body to focus a variety of social, political, and aesthetic concerns. Throughout the 1980s, she anatomized the inner workings of the human body in paperworks and sculptures, confronting such timeless issues as power and vulnerability, health and disease, birth and death. With this lithograph Smith broke new ground, utilizing the human exterior as a means of expression and incorporating herself as a model, both for the first time. JI

KIKI **SMITH**

Untitled (Hair)
1990
Color lithograph printed from nine stones and one plate on Mitsumata paper; edition 50/54; printed (by Douglas Volle) and published by Universal Limited Art Editions, West Islip, New York
36 x 36" (91.4 x 91.4 cm)
1994-63-1

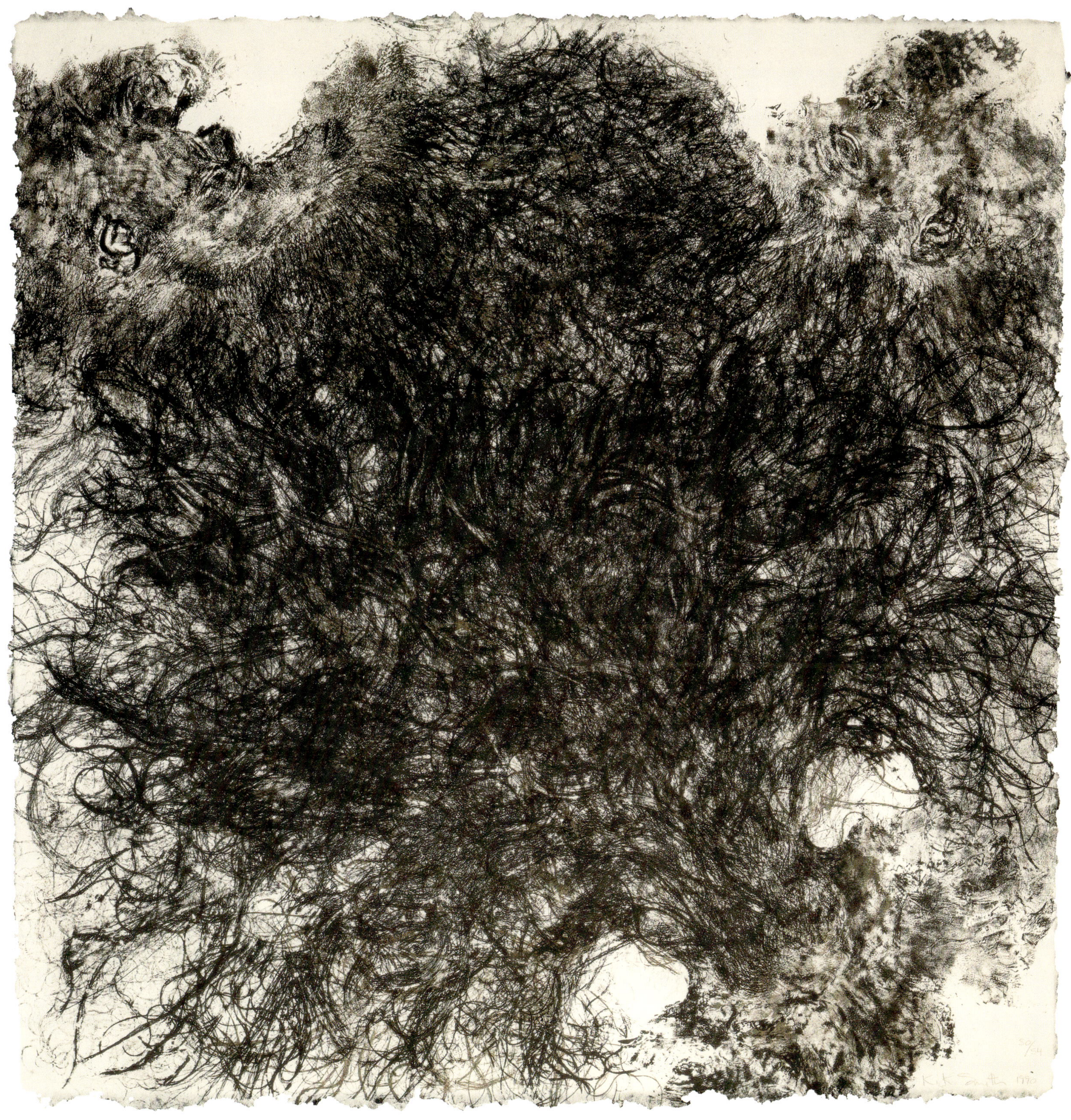

PAUL **THEK**

Paul Thek's works on paper form a lyrical counterpoint to the large-scale, site-specific, temporary installations that he created—primarily in Europe—from the 1960s through the mid-1980s, and for which he is best known today. Compounded of an astonishing variety of materials—sand, earth, oranges, onions, newspapers, a bathtub, letters, poems, live chickens, Christmas tree lights, an abandoned fishing boat, lumber, candles, and a red latex dwarf, to name but a few—and assembled with an apparent mad prodigality, these installations were actually subjected to an exacting and poetic control. Although none of the installations survives, other of Thek's works produced from the 1960s onward do remain, including several dozen oil, acrylic, ink, gouache, and gesso works on newspaper, as well as a number of sketchbooks and notebooks containing ruminations, pronouncements, quotations, diary entries, drafts of letters, drawings, and sketches. These personal notations expose the complexities of an artistic personality that embraced great extremes, from the holy sacrament to the drug-world counterculture, from the scatological to the sublime.

Dust and *Way Out* are two of six acrylic and gesso paintings on newspaper by Paul Thek purchased by the Philadelphia Museum of Art in 1992 that can function as a series. Produced during the last months of the artist's life, each work refers to an idea such as time, ephemerality, imprisonment, or mortality—subjects that obsessed Thek for much of his career. Words reinforce the symbolism in several of the drawings: in one, the phrase "time is a river" is splashed across a rushing cascade of blue paint; in another, "the face of GOD" is lettered beneath the hands of a clock. Thek's preoccupation with time relates to his conviction that technological advancement and the linear progress of history serve to separate humanity from its inherent mystical communion with nature and from its sense of "mythical time." Subjects such as clocks, newspapers, calendars, and astronomical phenomena symbolized for Thek broad concepts regarding the human condition in all its paradoxes: creativity and destructiveness, imprisonment and liberation, life and death, eternity and temporality, good and evil, reason and mysticism. Although such concerns pervaded a quarter century of Thek's artistic production, the idea of transience is especially poignant in these newspaper paintings, made when the artist had so little time left to live. AP

Dust
1988
Acrylic and gesso on newspaper
21 1/4 x 27 3/8" (54 x 69.5 cm)
1992-128-1

Way Out
1988
Acrylic and gesso on newspaper
21 1/4 x 27 3/8" (54 x 69.5 cm)
1992-127-1

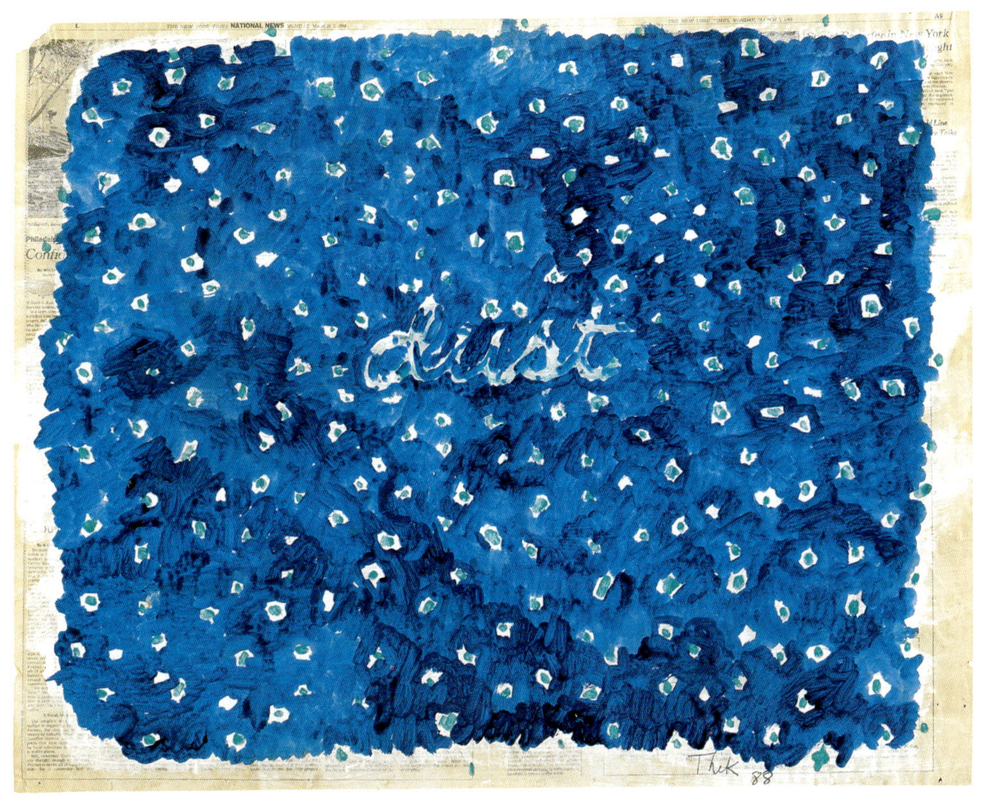
dust

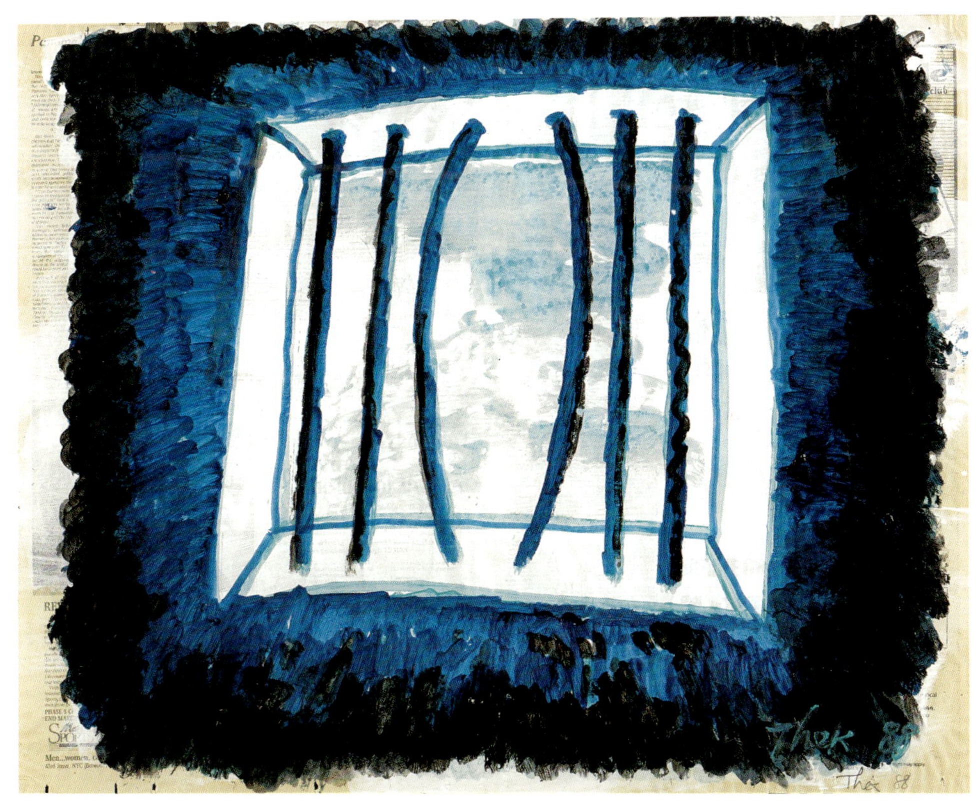

Rosemarie Trockel's *White Carrot* portfolio consists of three mysteriously related objects: a group of ten prints, a porcelain cast of an icicle, and a photograph of the process of casting it—an event that took place at 12,000 feet in the Engadine (Switzerland), where the artist and the publisher Peter Blum weathered the elements to select it. As in much of Trockel's work, images from obscure sources have been reworked and transformed in new techniques and combinations. Oppositions abound between clashing art historical influences, black and white, rough and smooth, geometric and irregular, and of course male and female, an opposition most clearly evident in the icicle and its "female" mold.

A sense of obscurity pervades the etchings, whose images are all but illegible, though this effect scarcely matters because of the sensuous textures and spare compositional elegance of the works. Smooth, rectangular, black aquatints are positioned irregularly on larger rectangles of white paper onto which Trockel has photographically transferred topographical maps of Europe. The etched images of the maps are so deeply bitten that they are embossed into the paper, creating rough textures that provide an evocative ground for the aquatints. As abstract forms, the dark, finite rectangles on the rough ground recall Kasimir Malevich's geometric compositions—an intentional reference to one of Trockel's favorite sources—although closer inspection reveals scenes embedded within the darkness. Each of the aquatints contains an image taken from different magazine articles about weather conditions such as snow, ice, wind, and fog, creating a romantic character that the artist says reflects her interest in German Romanticism. IHS

ROSEMARIE **TROCKEL**

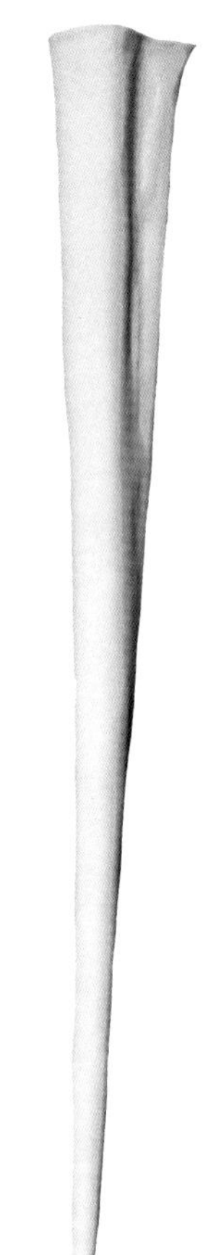

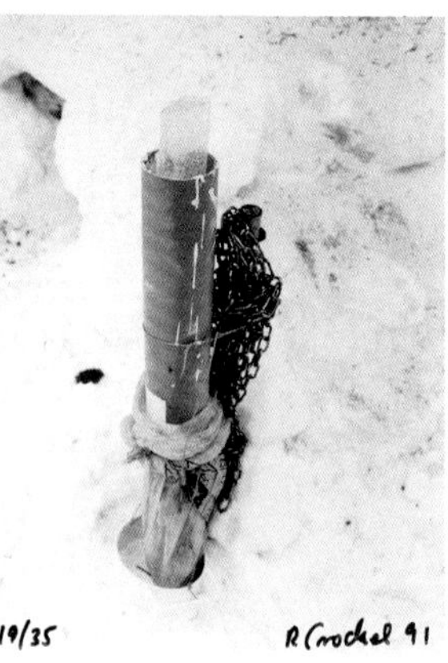

White Carrot
1991
Portfolio containing ten prints, one photograph, and one porcelain object (icicle); edition 19/35

Photogravure, aquatint, and embossing on Swiss Zerkall paper
$21\frac{1}{4} \times 14\frac{7}{8}$" (54 x 37.8 cm) sheets
Printed by Peter Kneubühler, Zurich

Gelatin silver print
$9\frac{1}{2} \times 7\frac{1}{8}$" (24.1 x 18.1 cm)
Printed by Wolfgang Burat, Cologne

Unglazed porcelain
$20\frac{3}{4}$"(52.7 cm) high
Cast under the supervision of Hans Jürgen Schönenberg, Selb, Germany

Published by Peter Blum Edition, New York
1991-148-1a–l

Javier Vallhonrat explores the ontology of the photograph as icon and object, as a two-dimensional surface representing multidimensional space, and as a temporal relic. *Untitled, No. 15 (Ice)*, from his *Precarious Objects* series, is replete with the tensions that characterize this body of work. The ice cube, a small object that melts to nothing as it performs its purpose, is presented as monumental in scale and fixed into permanency. This monumentality is underscored by the solidity of the aluminum support to which the photograph is adhered. Paradoxically, when installed, this seemingly massive object is propped on a thin ledge that appears barely capable of supporting its weight.

In a further paradox, the ice cube appears to melt before our eyes, making our own position precarious as we imagine the ensuing flood. Held within the relentless square image, the fluid shape of the ice cube is intensified. No part of it is exactly in focus except, oddly, some areas of reflected light, so that the least substantial elements of the image thus become the most definitive. The surface of the photograph at close range has a lustrous and sensuous quality—an objectness separate entirely from the representation of the ice cube. MC

JAVIER **VALLHONRAT**

Untitled, No. 15 (Ice),
from the *Precarious Objects* series
1993–94
Chromogenic color print mounted on aluminum, edition 3/3
49 3/8 x 49 3/8 x 1/2" (125.4 x 125.4 x 1.3 cm)
1995-45-1

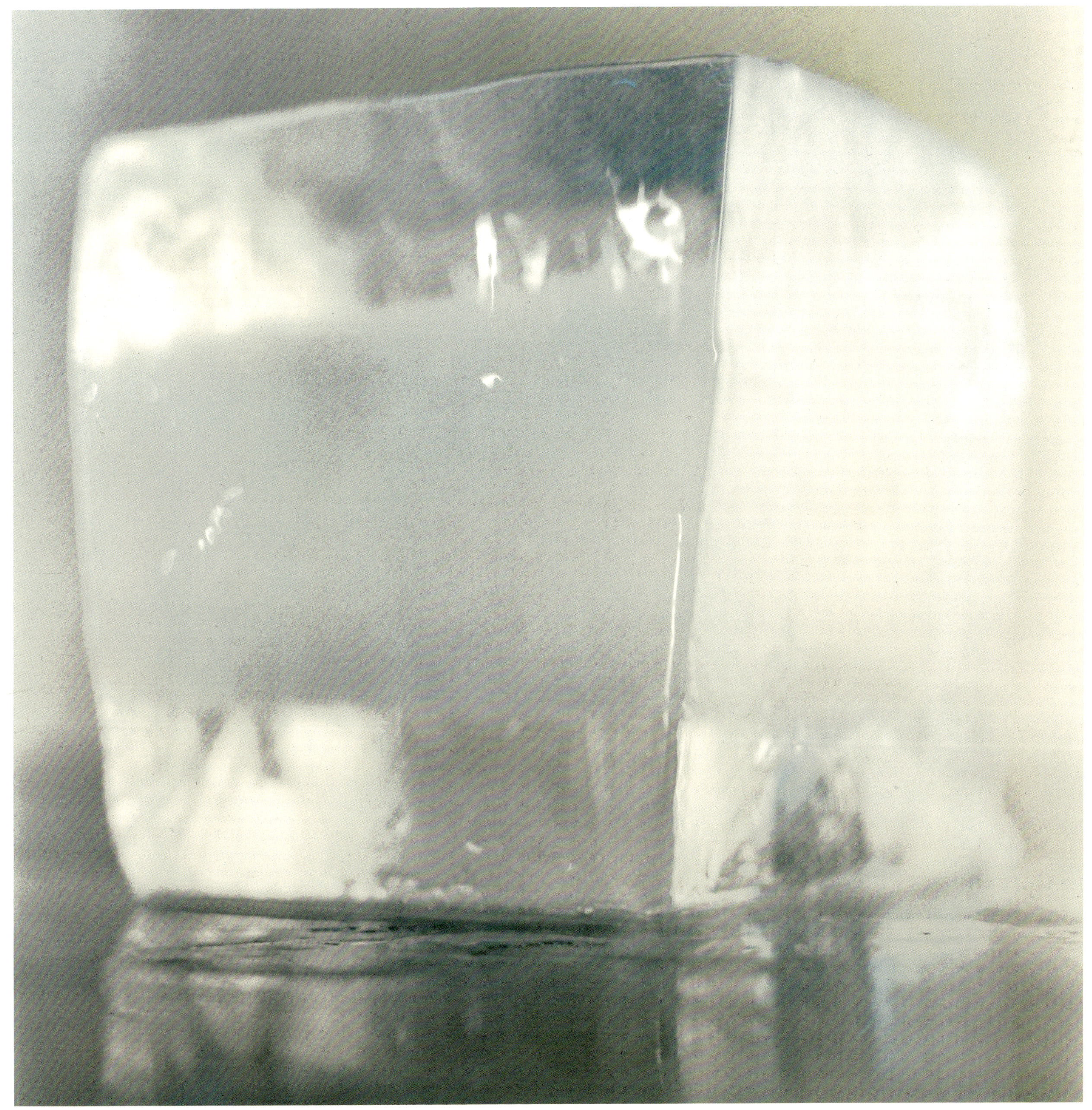

WILLIAM **WEGMAN**

Like a number of artists in the 1960s and 1970s who felt the burden of an overwhelming legacy of painting and who were loosely grouped as Conceptual artists, William Wegman turned to photography to find a form of making art that had the spark of something new. He was among the first artists using photography to take his cue from Marcel Duchamp, eschewing any pretension to the aesthetics of fine art photography and using the medium in a deliberately banal way to explore ideas contained in visual puns, palindromes, perceptual anomalies and ambiguities, and word-play. It quickly became apparent that Wegman was funny, often at his own expense. Wegman himself participated in the scenarios he staged for photographs and videos, frequently using his body as the vehicle for his jokes. After acquiring a weimaraner named Man Ray in 1970, Wegman began including the dog in his work. By 1979, when he made his first 20-by-24-inch Polaroid prints, the artist had been completely upstaged. His work with Man Ray and later Fay Ray, the dog in *Back/Front/Top*, has been continually witty and inventive, a long-running vaudeville act in which the butt of the joke steals the show.

Back/Front/Top is a magician's trick with Fay, the magician's assistant, improbably squeezed into a small box. Is she the famous lady sawn in half, or is she two dogs side by side in a bottomless box? Wegman has often parodied other works of art and art movements, and this piece is reminiscent of Surrealist artist Man Ray's *Auto-Portrait* (1933), which was created at a time when the artist felt himself misunderstood and persecuted by criticism. The dog in the rough-hewn wood box, with her mournful expression and neutral brown coloring, recalls the earlier work, in which the artist's bronze head was packed into a similar box as if for shipment. *Back/Front/Top* pokes sly fun at the self-indulgence of pessimism, morbid introspection, and depression. MC

Back/Front/Top
1989
Dye diffusion transfer print
24 x 20" (61 x 50.8 cm)
1990-16-1

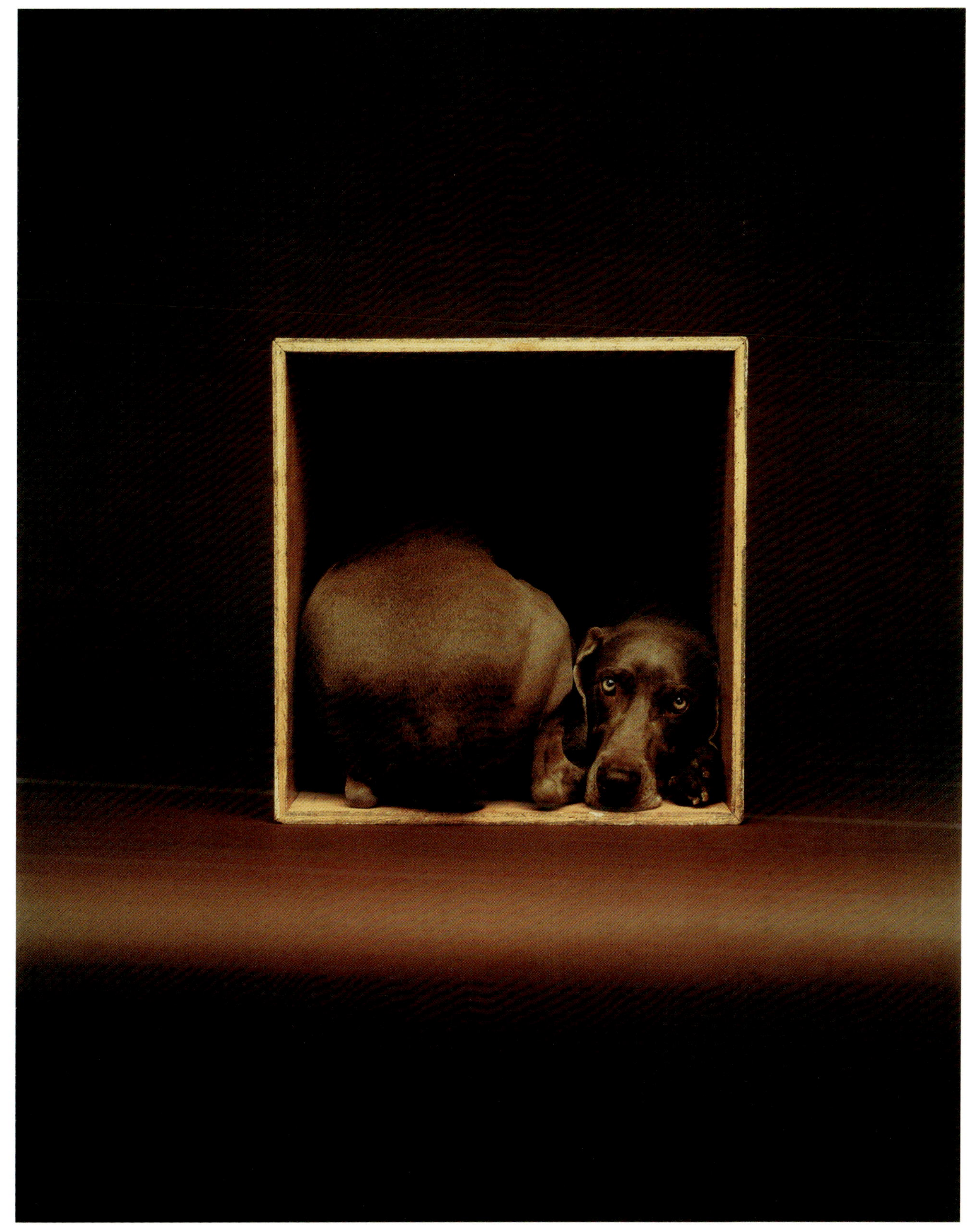

Neil Winokur's *Self-Portrait* is a loose constellation of autobiographical photographs of the artist and his possessions from childhood to the present. These deadpan mugshots and object "portraits," like Hollywood promotions with their supersaturated color backgrounds, open up the whole question of photographic portraiture by avoiding, at all costs, any attempt at psychological content. Just as it is fundamentally impossible to judge the nature of a stranger from external appearance alone, these works underscore the futility of determining character and personality from photographs. Photographic portraits can convey emotional states, expressive gestures, and a sense of liveliness, but these should not be mistaken for essential character. They can be primarily iconic and posed, as in the work of Robert Mapplethorpe, Richard Avedon, and August Sander. They can incorporate props indicative of the sitter's profession or interests, as in the work of Arnold Newman, Bill Brandt, and Cecil Beaton.

Winokur's work is a hybrid of the iconic and the environmental. Basically, its interpretation depends upon what the viewer brings to it, which is all that can really happen with any portrait. In a way, *Self-Portrait* becomes a mutual and congenial biography including both Winokur and his audience. Winokur applies a broad stroke of universality and brings a lighthearted sense of humor to this work. The individual objects in the portrait (slide rule and hash pipe, Butch hair wax and *On the Road*) not only reflect Winokur's specific experience, but build a generational portrait as well. MC

NEIL **WINOKUR**

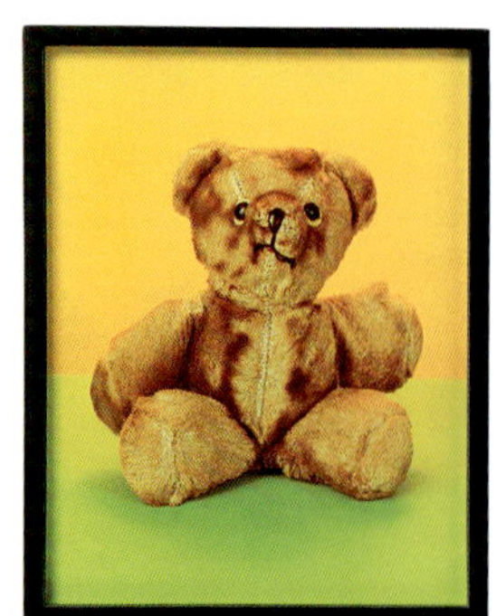

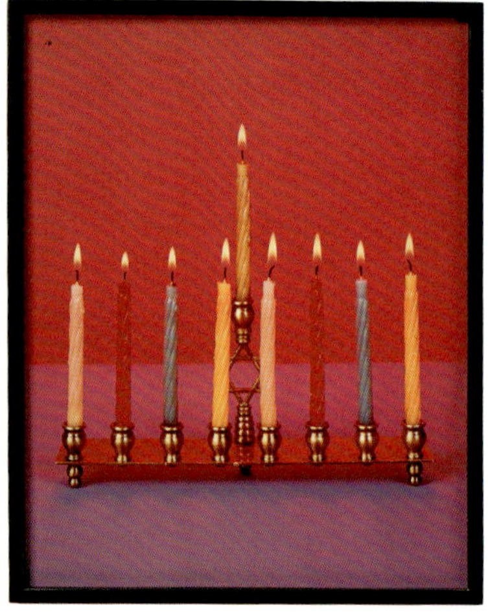

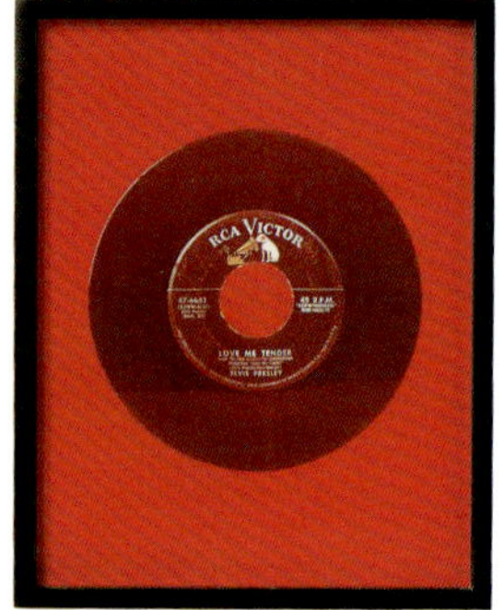

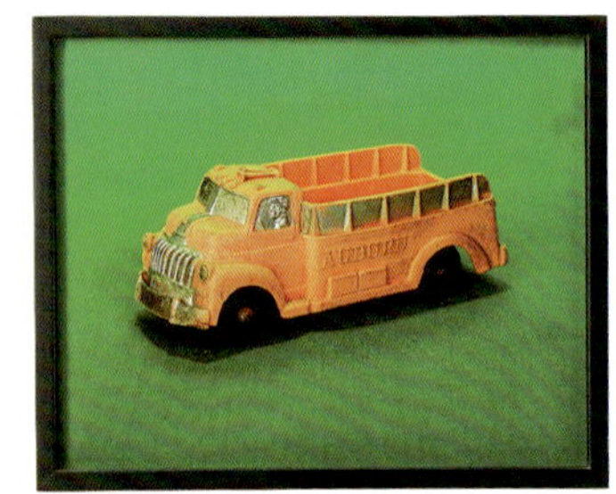

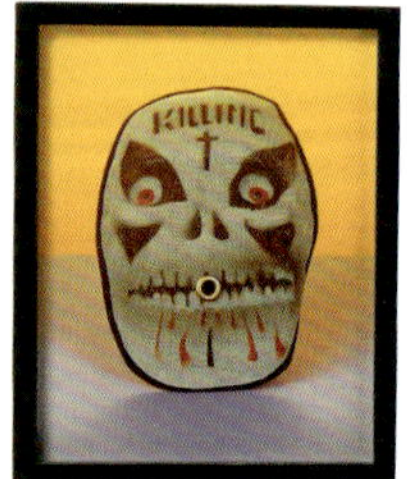

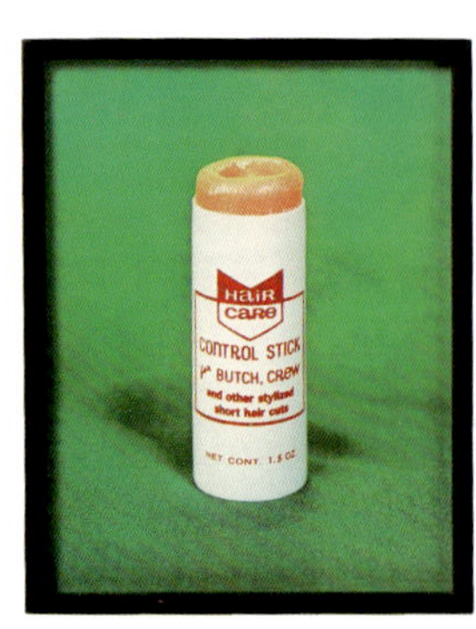

Self-Portrait
1990
Seventeen of a series of forty silver dye bleach prints; edition of 5
8 x 10" (20.3 x 25.4 cm), 11 x 14" (27.9 x 35.6 cm), 16 x 20" (40.6 x 50.8 cm) sheets
1991-149-1–17

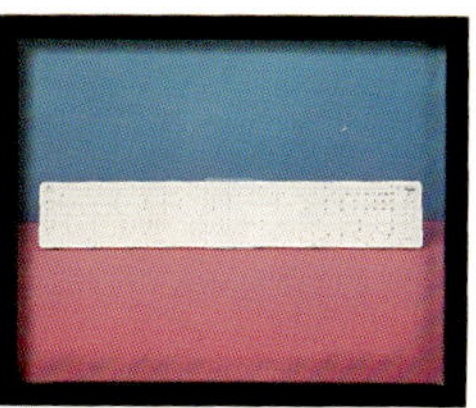

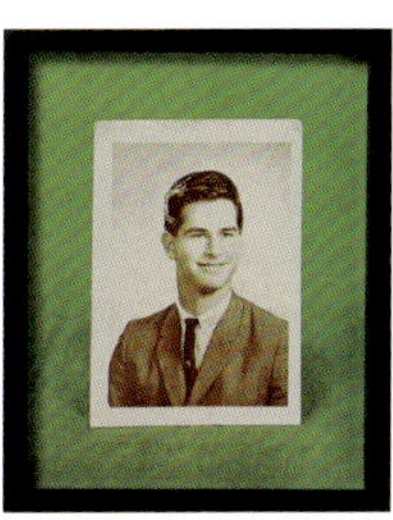

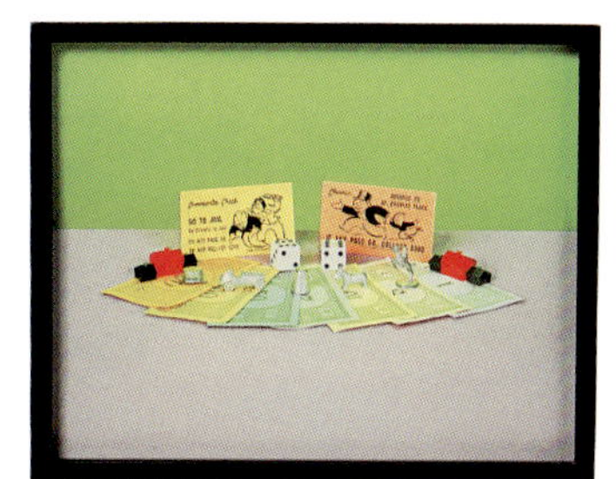

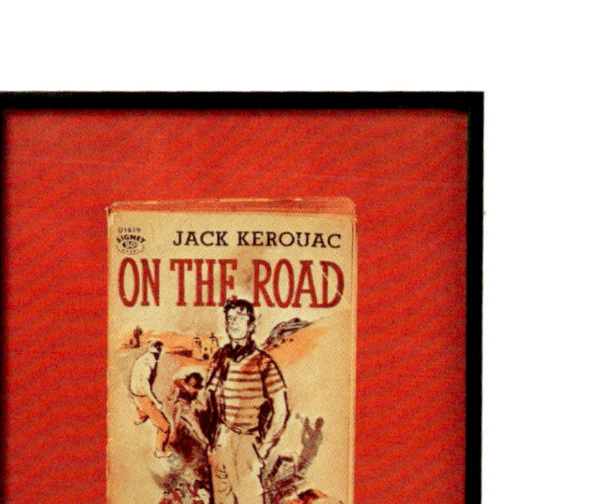
JACK KEROUAC
ON THE ROAD
A SIGNET BOOK • Complete and Unabridged

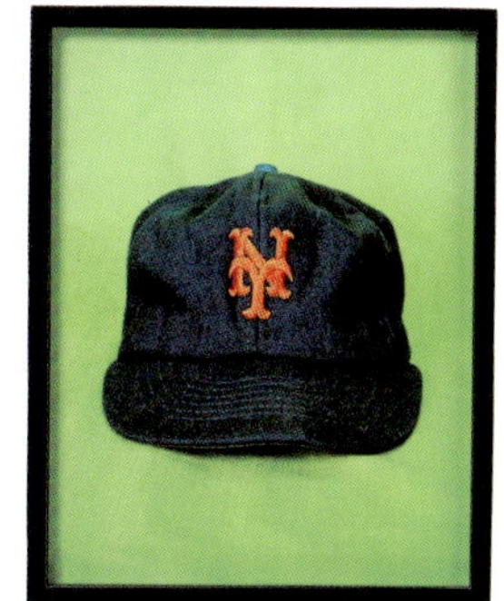

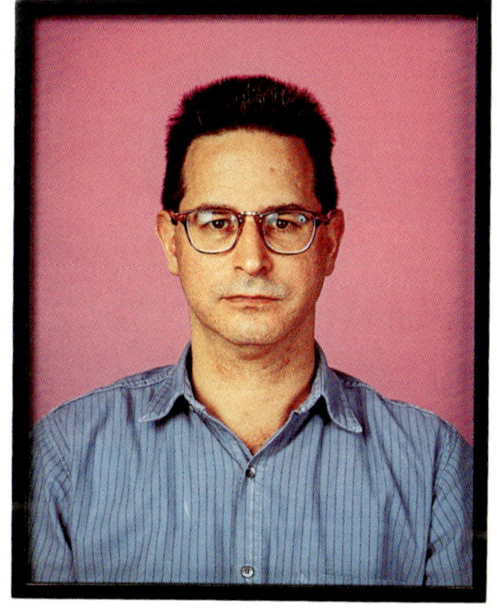

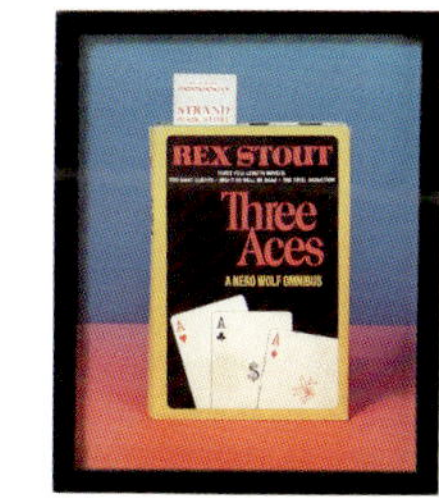
REX STOUT
Three Aces

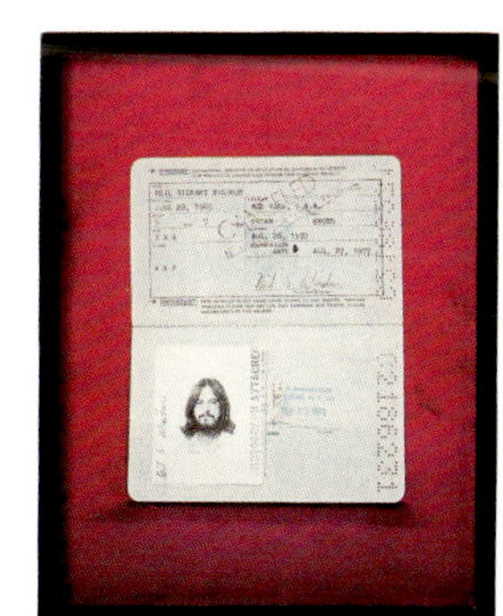

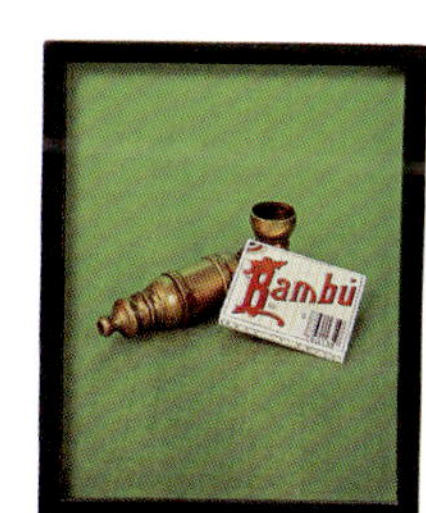
Bambú

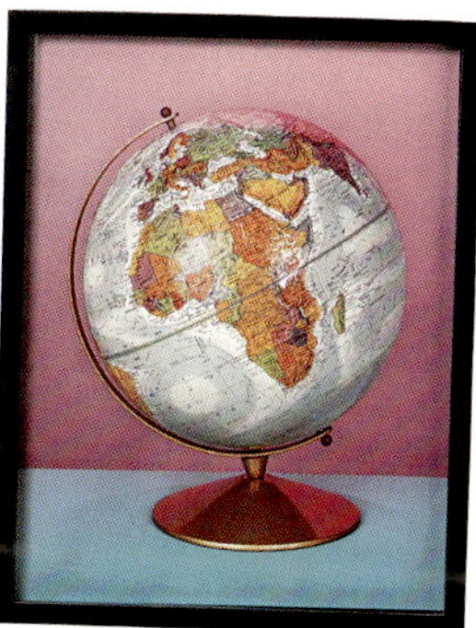

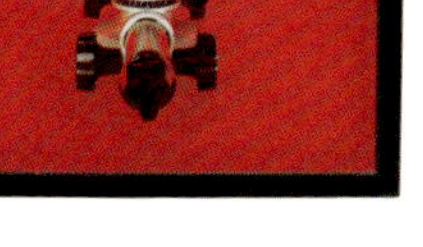

ROBIN **WINTERS**

A performance artist who once participated in a Whitney Biennial exhibition dressed as a bear, Robin Winters retains—and imparts—a childlike sense of wonder in homespun scenes of imaginary derring-do. In *The Seed Multipliers*, the artist lays out fifteen whimsical vignettes in five rows, comic-book style, and flanks them with a pair of panels to create a three-part work that recalls an older format—that of the compartmented triptych painting used for nonverbal narrative purposes in European churches during the Middle Ages and Renaissance.

An inveterate storyteller, Winters will readily spell out the details of the adventures he depicts in individual scenes, as in the middle square at the left, which he describes as a man who has "freaked out because he's worked at a rocket factory too long."[1] But the artist is just as quick to admit that his stories change from telling to telling—always the case with folktales—and he leaves us free to divine our own meanings. In each of the two side panels, five disembodied female heads—based on photographs published in *Vogue* magazine—provide an audience for the central action. These smiling dreamgirls seem to have drifted up from some watery depth to the blue-green surface, where they are framed by looping borders of miniature faces spawned by the unconscious. The title of this work, borrowed from a magazine article on heirloom roses, alludes to the mysterious forces underlying all creative enterprise. J I

The Seed Multipliers
1988
Etching and color linocut printed from fifteen plates and fifteen blocks on five sheets of Japanese kozo paper (center panel), and color lithograph and woodcut with applied color and bronzing powder on Japanese Uda paper (side panels); edition 3/25; printed (by David Calkins and David Keister) and published by Echo Press, Bloomington, Indiana
56⅝ x 31⅛" (143.8 x 79.1 cm) center panel
57 x 12¾" (144.8 x 32.4 cm) side panels
1989-15-1a,b,c

1. Quoted in Holland Carter, "Robin Winters: Performing in Print," *Print Collector's Newsletter*, vol. 19, no. 4 (September–October 1988), p. 144.

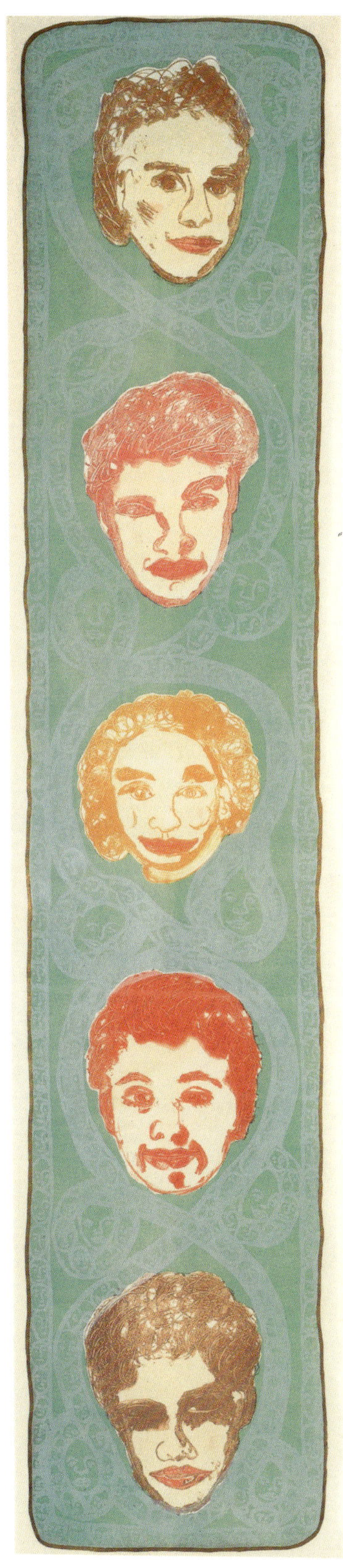

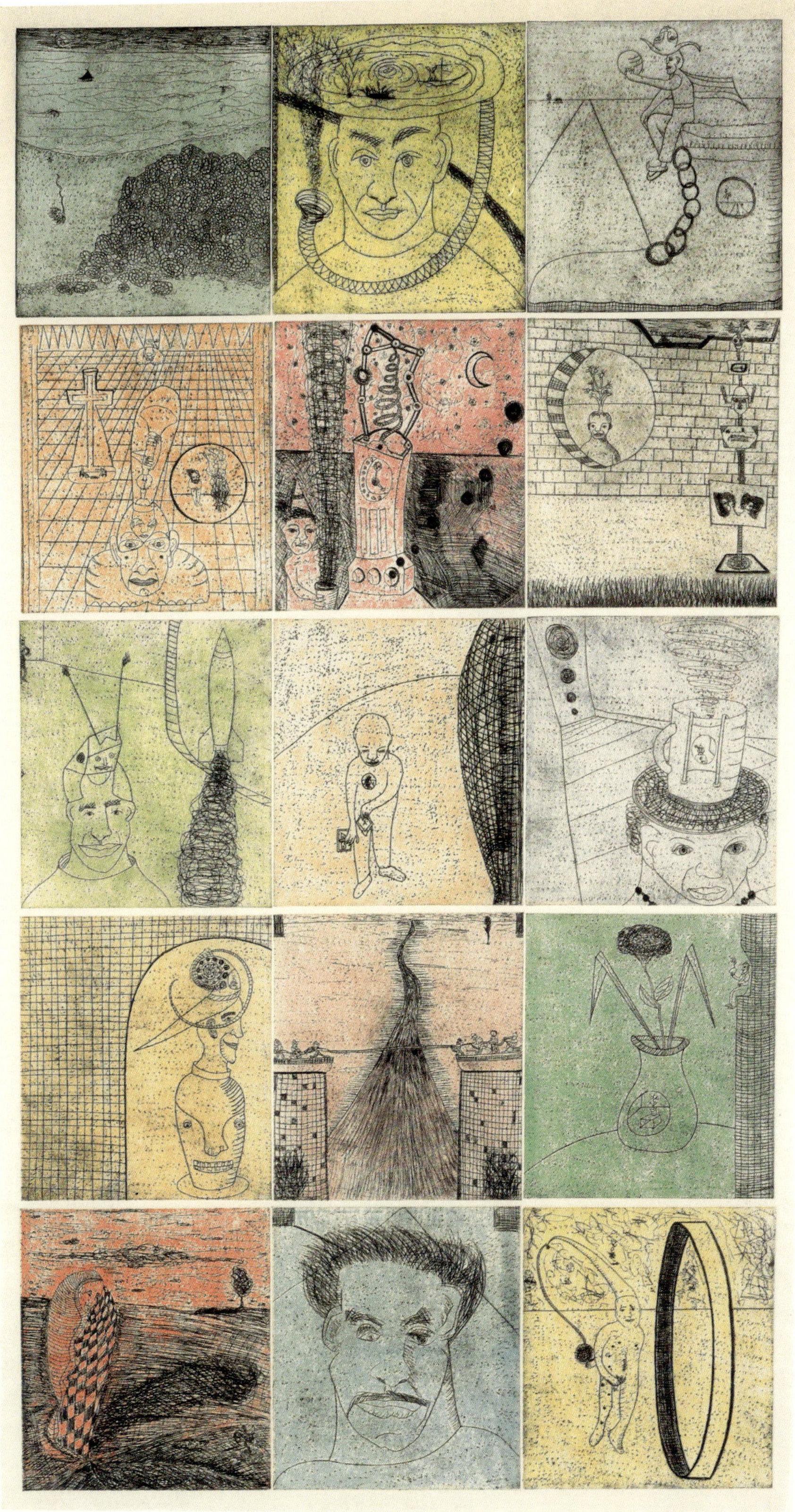

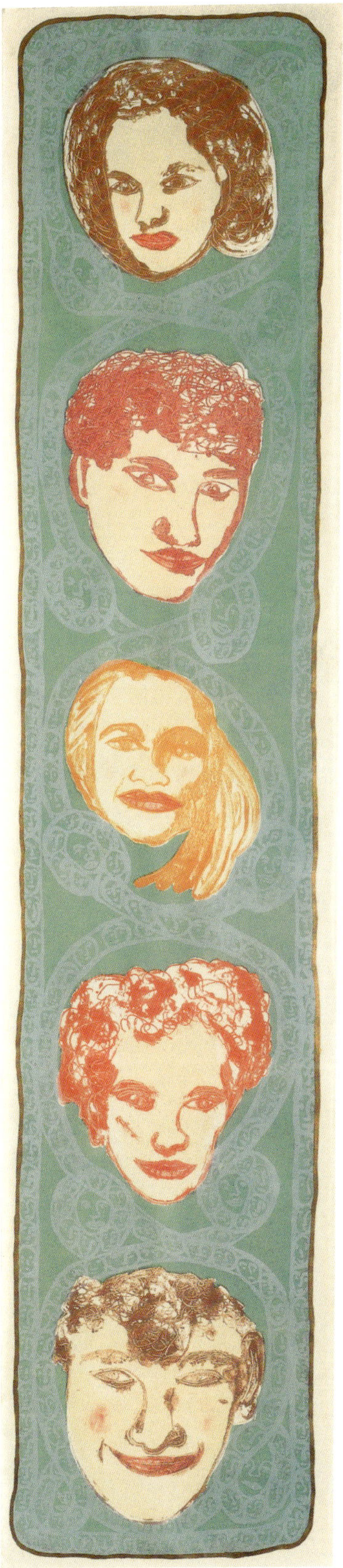

CHRISTOPHER **WOOL**

Christopher Wool uses commercially produced decorative stamps in a vine pattern to apply a shiny black paint to sheets of glossy paper or aluminum. The combination of the commercial process with the synthetic-appearing surface gives the work a smooth, manufactured look. Through his use of the patterned stamps, Wool has nearly eliminated from this painting any trace of thought or deliberation. And yet, he has provided ample evidence of his working process in the areas of unevenly stamped paint and in the buildup of paint in places where the successive stampings join to create an imprecise grid pattern. In addition, the two layers of stamped vine patterns have been overlapped, adding some depth and complexity to the overall composition.

Wool's wallpaper-like paintings on paper or aluminum have provoked critical speculation of the most complex and weighty order. Is he challenging worn-out concepts of originality with his use of commercial decorative stamps? Is the banality of his commercially produced patterns a comment upon the exhaustion of painted imagery? Is he using the stamps as a way of exerting control over the randomness of artistic freedom of decision? All of these questions evoke issues already confronted by some of the most august artists of this century, including Marcel Duchamp, Jackson Pollock, and Jasper Johns. Wool himself has little to say on these matters. Yet despite their apparent meaninglessness and eminent inscrutability, his works have a presence that is both deliberate and powerful, which is undoubtedly why they have provoked so much discussion. IHS

Untitled
1991
Alkyd stamped on two sheets of paper
52 x 40" (132.1 x 101.6 cm)
1993-18-1

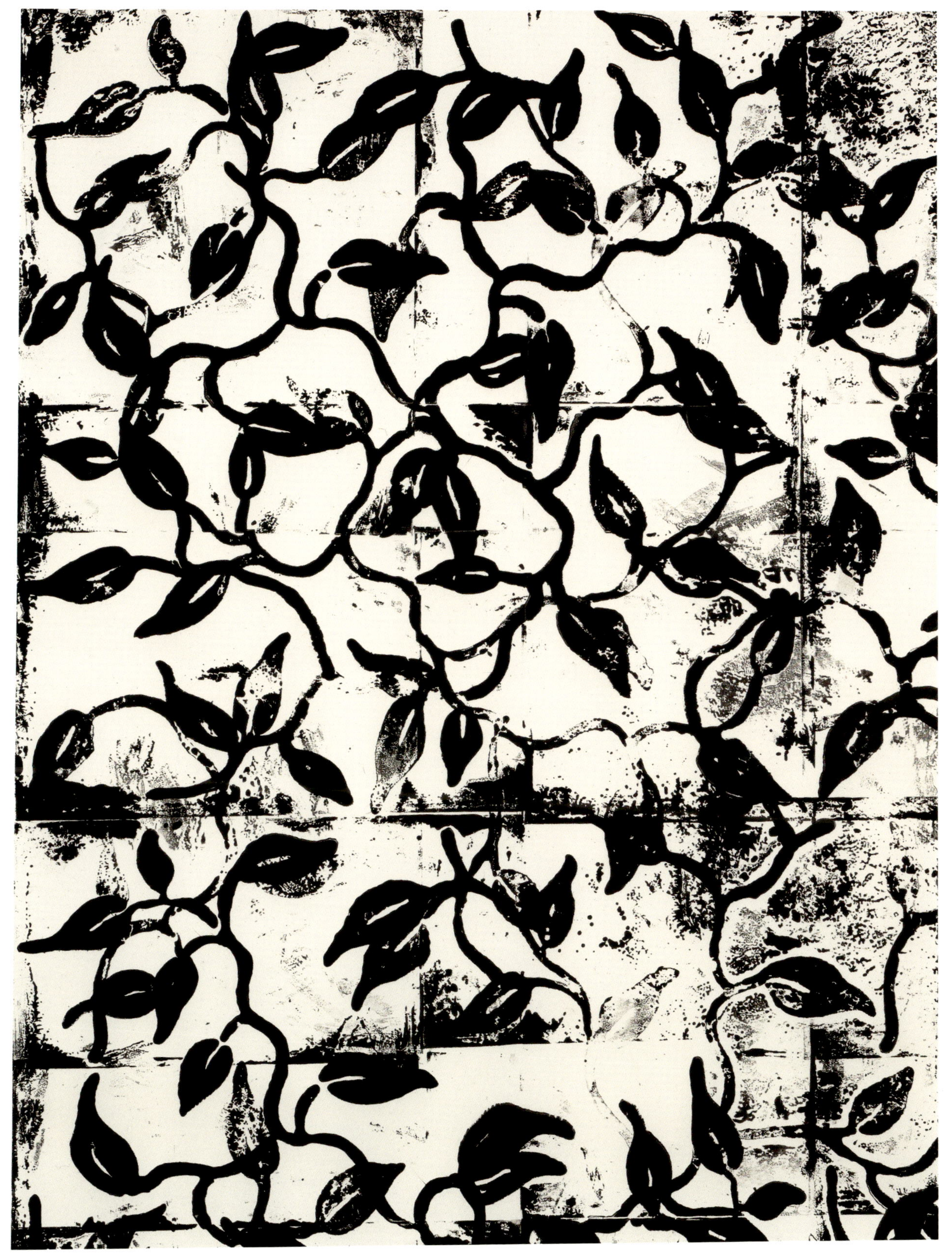

BIOGRAPHIES OF THE ARTISTS

by Susan Dackerman

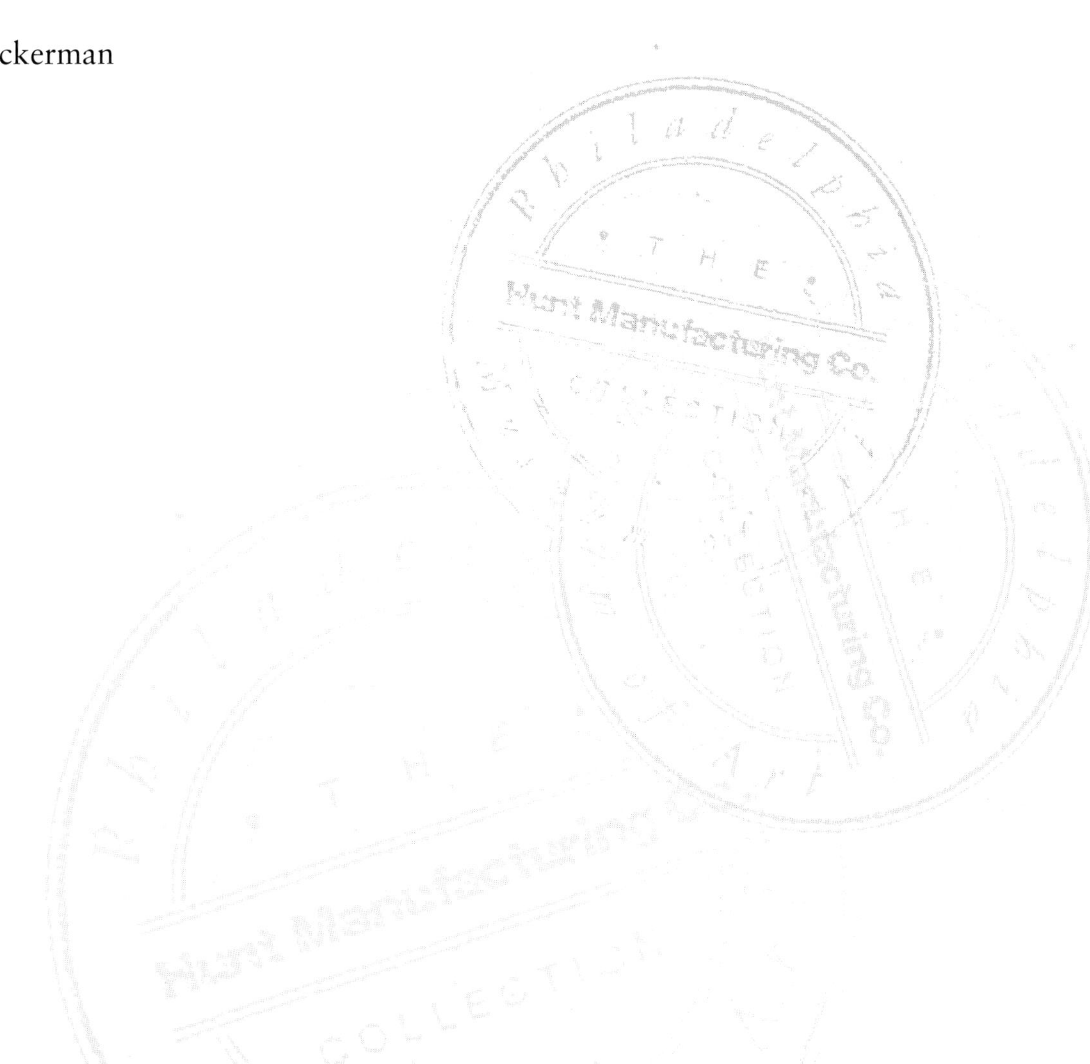

JOSÉ BEDIA (pp. 12–13)

Born 1959, Havana, Cuba
Studied Instituto Superior de Arte, Havana, 1981
Resides Miami, Florida

In 1990, just nine years after he and a group of other young artists struggled to convince the Ministry of Culture to allow them to exhibit their avant-garde work in a Havana storefront, José Bedia was chosen to represent Cuba at the Venice Biennale. Bedia gained international acclaim at the Latin American Biennials held in Havana in 1984 and 1986, and was the Cuban representative to the 1987 São Paulo Biennial. His work was also featured in the 1989 exhibition *Magiciens de la Terre*, at the Musée National d'Art Moderne, Centre Georges Pompidou, in Paris. Born just five days after Fidel Castro took power, Bedia is a true offspring of the socialist regime. His artistic training, though traditional, was provided by the state, as was his access to exhibition spaces and jobs in national museums. However, because of the difficult social and economic conditions under which artists in Cuba now live, Bedia and numerous other "generation of the '80s" artists recently left that country.

Bedia's work reflects his extensive knowledge of and interest in indigenous cultures, as well as the syncretic Afro-Cuban culture of his own country. He travels widely, collecting both ancient and contemporary artifacts of native cultures, which he keeps in his living and studio spaces and sometimes incorporates into his work. As an initiated priest of the Afro-Cuban religion of *palo monte*, he is deeply engaged by its myths and fascinated by their fundamental similarity to the myths of other aboriginal cultures. Through the modernist expression of these ancient mythologies, Bedia attempts to construct a picture of Cuban identity in a post-colonial state.

Reference Melissa E. Feldman. *José Bedia: De Donde Vengo*. Philadelphia: Institute of Contemporary Art, University of Pennsylvania, 1994.

ZEKE BERMAN (pp. 14–15)

Born 1951, New York
Studied Philadelphia College of Art, B.F.A., 1972
Teaches Yale University, New Haven, Connecticut
School of Visual Arts, New York
Fordham University at Lincoln Center, New York
Resides New York

Zeke Berman's formal training as a sculptor is evident in the meticulously assembled constructions of wood, newspaper, clay, and other ordinary objects he photographs. Berman taught himself the mechanics of photography in the years following his last sculpture exhibition in 1973. The first formal show of his photographs was held in 1980 at the Everson Museum in Syracuse, New York, and he has continued to work in photography since then. Berman explores in his photographs the possibilities of reducing three-dimensional objects to a two-dimensional plane; he attempts to expose the cognitive processes that give meaning to the viewer's perception of the image on the flat surface. His interest in theories of perception originated while he was in school, and his reading in Gestalt psychology has influenced both his choice of subjects and their presentation. In recent years, Berman has been photographing objects with linear qualities, like wire and yarn, in order to appropriate for photography the attributes of drawing. Since 1980, Berman has had solo exhibitions at various museums in this country and in Europe, including the Cleveland Museum of Art, the Art Institute of Chicago, and the Museum of Modern Art in Bern, Switzerland. He has been the recipient of numerous grants, including an NEA fellowship.

Reference Debra Heimerdinger. *Optiks: Zeke Berman*. San Francisco: The Friends of Photography, 1991.

MEL BOCHNER (pp. 16–17)

Born 1940, Pittsburgh, Pennsylvania
Studied Carnegie Institute of Technology, Pittsburgh, B.F.A., 1962
Resides New York

Mel Bochner has been exhibiting his work since the late 1960s. He received a traditional training at the Carnegie Institute, learning to draw from still lifes, plaster casts, and human models. In his early work, however, Bochner disregarded these lessons, producing drawings and photographic pieces that incorporated words, numbers, and shapes. These highly theoretical works, executed in what has been called Bochner's "analytical" style, visually explored the complex relationships between language, thought, and sight, recalling the philosophy classes the artist took at Northwestern University in 1963, when it was the center of phenomenological study in the United States.

In 1973, after admiring the colors and architectural integration of trecento frescoes in Italy, Bochner began to paint directly on walls. He also ceased producing the theoretical language pieces that same year, acknowledging the difficulty of interpretation for the viewer. Through his wall paintings, Bochner sought to resolve his conceptualist aversion to the "objectness" of art. Ironically, he was eventually frustrated by the impermanence of the wall paintings and sought a more lasting medium. In 1982, he began painting on canvas, and his early paintings on canvas demonstrate an unprecedented interest in gesture. By the end of the decade, however, Bochner had returned to the geometry and perspectival grids of his early work, although these new works, on paper and on canvas, have more weight and volume, the result of a year spent looking at paintings and architecture in Rome. Bochner has participated in exhibitions at the Albertina in Vienna and at the Museum of Fine Arts in Boston. In 1995, the Yale University Art Gallery organized a retrospective of his early work.

References *Mel Bochner: 1973–1985*. Essay by Elaine A. King. Pittsburgh: Carnegie-Mellon University Press, 1985.

Richard Field. *Mel Bochner: Thought Made Visible 1966–1973*. New Haven, Conn.: Yale University Art Gallery, 1995.

DOVE BRADSHAW (pp. 18–19)

Born 1949, New York
Studied Boston Museum School of Fine Arts, B.F.A., 1973
Resides New York

Dove Bradshaw's work is typically interpreted in relation to her longstanding association with John Cage, but her first mature work was inspired by the art of Marcel Duchamp. As a child, Bradshaw annually visited the Philadelphia Museum of Art, where she was impressed by the look and elegance of Duchamp's representations of machines. Her work of the late 1970s manifests conceptualist notions initiated by Duchamp in the first half of the century in such works as his "readymade" objects. In a 1976 piece called *Performance*, Bradshaw claimed a fire hose at the Metropolitan Museum of Art as her own art work by placing a wall label next to it, identifying herself as the artist. She similarly claimed a hygrometer, a device that measures the humidity in museum galleries. Bradshaw's burgeoning interest in the transmutations of materials over time is evident in the hygrometer piece and in an untitled piece from 1977 that documents the expected endurance—or lack of endurance—of all of the components of a matted and framed piece of newspaper in museum display conditions.

As a result of meeting Cage in 1977, Bradshaw's work became what she calls "more indeterminate." This is perhaps most apparent in her images that utilize silver and liver of sulfur (sulfurated potash). In 1985, Bradshaw began to apply silver leaf to small sheets of paper, and then pour liver of sulfur on them to oxidize the silver. The results are unpredictable, dependent upon the amount of moisture in the air. Even after the initial chemical reaction, the surfaces continue to change in response to atmospheric conditions. She has since created large canvases using the same technique. Bradshaw's interest in uncertainty is also made apparent in her recently produced first film, entitled *Indeterminacy*, in which she examines the changing states of water and stone. The transformation of stone is as well the subject of her most recent sculptural work, in which pyrite is applied to large blocks of marble, unpredictably marking the stone. These works are intended for outdoor installation, as water and humidity alter their appearance.

Bradshaw has had numerous solo exhibitions at the Sandra Gering Gallery in New York, and her work has been included in exhibitions at the Art Institute of Chicago and the Museum of Modern Art in New York. In 1993, her work appeared in *Rolywholyover A Circus*, an exhibition based on the life and work of John Cage, with whom she became good friends. Since 1984, Bradshaw has also served as an artistic advisor to the Merce Cunningham Dance Company.

Reference *Dove Bradshaw: Works, 1969–1993*. New York: Sandra Gering Gallery, 1993.

JOHN CAGE (pp. 20–21)

Born 1912, Los Angeles
Studied Pomona College, Claremont, California, 1928–30
Died 1992, New York

Although John Cage promised his teacher Arnold Schoenberg in the mid-1930s that he would devote himself entirely to music and forsake his other artistic inclinations, Cage returned to the visual arts in 1969 when he made *Not Wanting to Say Anything About Marcel*, a series of plexigrams and lithographs produced to commemorate Marcel Duchamp's death. Cage's renewed interest in visual mediums was further advanced by an invitation in 1978 to make etchings at Crown Point Press, then in Oakland, California. Until his death, Cage returned to Crown Point at least once each year to produce a series of prints. During those years he also experimented with drawings and watercolors at the Mountain Lake Workshop in Virginia.

Cage was born in Los Angeles in 1912. After attending Pomona College for two years, he set off for Europe to compose music, write poetry, and paint. Upon his return to the United States, he resolved to pursue his musical studies seriously. By the early 1940s, he was regarded as a prominent avant-garde musician, having composed for modern dance troupes, invented the "prepared" piano (a technique in which strips of cardboard and other materials are inserted between the strings), and performed at various venues, including the Museum of Modern Art in New York. In 1948, he began teaching during the summers at Black Mountain College in North Carolina. It was there in 1952 that the first "Happening" took place, a collaborative multimedia presentation put forth by Cage, choreographer Merce Cunningham, painter Robert Rauschenberg, and others. After 1950, Cage's artistic endeavors were influenced by his study of Zen Buddhism and his attention to the *I Ching*, an ancient Chinese book of divination. The *I Ching* dictated the use of "chance operations" in his work, a means of working in a calculated but nondeliberate manner.

Though Cage is best known as an avant-garde composer, his interests also encompassed dance (he served as the musical director of the Merce Cunningham Dance Company from 1944–66), the study of fungi (he was one of the founders of the New York Mycological Society), theater, chess, and macrobiotic cooking, to name but a few. Cage's philosophy and random musings are related in his numerous books, including one on mushrooms. In 1988–89, Cage delivered the Charles Eliot Norton Lectures at Harvard University. He died in August of 1992, a month shy of his eightieth birthday.

Reference *Rolywholyover A Circus*. Edited by Russell Ferguson. Los Angeles: Museum of Contemporary Art; New York: Rizzoli, 1993.

PETER CAMPUS (pp. 22–23)

Born 1937, New York
Studied Ohio State University, B.S., 1960
Teaches New York University
Resides New York

Eleven years after obtaining an undergraduate degree in psychology, Peter Campus started making art seriously. He experimented with painting and photography before making his first artistic videos in 1971, but he had no formal artistic training in any medium. His previous ten years of experience in the film and television industry was instrumental in his decision to focus on video, then a relatively new and unexplored field. In the early 1970s, Campus had a series of exhibitions in which video cameras projected images of the spectators onto the gallery walls, a technique which transformed the viewer from a detached spectator to a participant in the process of artistic production. These installations, the works for which Campus is best known, established the human figure as his primary subject. During the late 1970s, Campus started working from still images, projecting slides rather than video loops onto gallery walls, and in 1979, he had his first exhibition of still photographs.

With the evolution from the ephemeral medium of video installations to the more corporeal medium of photography, the primary subject of Campus's work also changed. In the late 1970s, Campus began photographing landscape subjects—buildings, tunnels, and bridges—and eventually natural subjects such as trees, rocks, and leaves. Although his interest in photographing natural subjects has persisted, since 1989 he has been modifying his photographs through computer manipulation. Campus is regarded as a pioneer in the field of computer-manipulated photography, and his work is often featured in exhibitions that spotlight this theme. He also participated in the 1993 Whitney Biennial.

Reference *Peter Campus: Selected Works 1973–1987*. Essays by David S. Rubin and Judith Tannenbaum. Reading, Pa.: Freedman Gallery, Albright College, 1987.

WILLIE COLE (pp. 24–25)

Born 1955, Somerville, New Jersey
Studied Boston University School of Fine Arts, 1974–75
The School of Visual Arts, New York, B.F.A., 1976
The Arts Students League, New York, 1976–78
Resides Newark, New Jersey

Willie Cole has humorously characterized his work as "archaeological ethnographic Dada."[1] By archaeological, he means that he makes his sculpture and works on paper with found objects—blow-dryers, shoes, window frames, irons, and ironing boards, detritus excavated from the streets and structures of Newark and New York. Although Cole generally produces numerous constructions with each of these materials, a technique that requires an ample supply of each object he uses, he never buys the materials new. Each item must have a previous history, and Cole leaves the symbols of that history, such as the grime or other markings, on his materials. While he strives to reinvent the meanings of these found objects within his constructions, he simultaneously seeks to preserve elements of their prior lives by incorporating aspects of their original uses into the content of the new work. For example, he describes his constructions made from blow-dryers, retrieved from a factory in the vicinity of his studio, as wind spirits. Works such as these represent an attempt to construct a new mythology from the objects of American material culture. The new mythology, however, is partially based upon the forms and folklore of African customs. Because Cole's artistic training was traditional, there are also resonances of other influences in his work, such as the found object assemblages of Picasso and the Dada constructions of Duchamp. His present ambition is to produce work that is more abstract. Cole's work has been featured in exhibitions at the Saint Louis Art Museum, the Studio Museum in Harlem, and the Newark Museum in New Jersey.

1. Quoted in Elizabeth A. Brown, "Social Studies: 4 + 4 Young Americans," *Allen Memorial Art Museum Bulletin*, vol. 44, no. 1 (1990), p. 18.

Reference *re:visioning the familiar*. Essay by Kenneth Miller and Traven Pelletier. Middletown, Conn.: Ezra and Cecile Zilkha Gallery, Wesleyan University, 1994.

GREGORY CREWDSON (pp. 26–27)

Born 1962, Brooklyn, New York
Studied State University of New York at Purchase, B.A., 1985
Yale University, School of Art, New Haven, Connecticut, M.F.A., 1988
Teaches Yale University
Resides Brooklyn

Gregory Crewdson's work was first publicly exhibited in the 1991 Museum of Modern Art show *Pleasures and Terrors of Domestic Comfort*. He has since had numerous solo exhibitions, including those at Luhring Augustine in New York and the Ruth Bloom Gallery in Los Angeles in 1995. Before attending the School of Art at Yale, Crewdson studied photography, American literature, and film at SUNY-Purchase, and his work is informed by a diverse array of sources from these fields, such as the filmmakers Alfred Hitchcock and Steven Spielberg, the landscape photographer Walker Evans, and the writer Raymond Carver. While at Yale, Crewdson photographed staged domestic scenes, enlisting unknown families and their homes as his models. Eventually dismayed by his own voyeurism into other people's lives, he began building intricate dioramas to photograph instead. Most of these tableaux are fanciful constructions of suburban homes and yards, painstakingly fabricated from an eclectic assortment of materials, including wood, wire, papier-mâché, dead butterflies, and taxidermically preserved birds and other animals. Crewdson's vision of suburban life, however, is not drawn from a childhood lived in the suburbs. He was raised and continues to live in the Park Slope section of Brooklyn.

Reference Hilarie M. Sheets. "The Burbs and the Bees." *Art News*, vol. 93 (October 1994), pp. 97–98.

GRENVILLE DAVEY (pp. 28–29)

Born 1961, Launceston, Cornwall
Studied Exeter College of Art and Design, 1981–82
Goldsmiths College, London, B.A., 1985
Resides London

In 1992, at the age of thirty-one, Grenville Davey was the unanticipated winner of the Turner Prize, an award sponsored in part by the Tate Gallery and presented to a British artist for the year's outstanding exhibition. Although Davey's work had been featured at the Stichting De Appel in Amsterdam, the Kunsthalle in Bern, and at two exhibitions at the Lisson Gallery in London, his work at the time was relatively unknown, especially to the American public. In 1994, Stuttgart's Württembergischer Kunstverein and the Musée Départemental de Rochechouart in Limoges jointly organized a major retrospective of his work.

Though he also makes prints and drawings, Davey is primarily known as a sculptor. As a student of Richard Deacon and Richard Wentworth, he has been identified with both minimalism and conceptualism, but his work defies strict categorization. His works often resemble the components of industrial life—manhole covers, airlocks, rails, and cylindrical tanks—but are not just found objects resituated within a gallery environment. The objects are usually fabricated to Davey's specifications from a variety of odd materials, such as spun steel, rubber, vinyl, and hardboard. Their often exaggerated scale, painted surfaces, and seemingly inappropriate placement within a gallery also challenge the viewer's perception of and relation to the objects.

References *Contemporary British Art in Print: The Publications of Charles Booth-Clibborn and His Imprint: The Paragon Press, 1986–95*. Edinburgh: Scottish National Gallery of Modern Art; London: The Paragon Press, 1995.

Grenville Davey. Essays by Tim Marlow and James Roberts. Limoges: Musée Départemental de Rochechouart; Stuttgart: Württembergischer Kunstverein Stuttgart, 1994.

RICHARD DEACON (pp. 30–31)

Born 1949, Bangor, Wales
Studied Somerset College of Art, Taunton, 1968–69
St. Martin's School of Art, London, 1969–72
Royal College of Art, London, 1974–77
Chelsea School of Art, London, 1977–78
Teaches Chelsea School of Art, London
Resides London

Richard Deacon was born in Wales to a mother who practiced medicine and a father who was a World War II aviator. Although he started his undergraduate degree at Somerset College in southwest England, he finished it in London at St. Martin's School of Art. Prior to entering the environmental media department at the Royal College of Art to pursue a graduate degree, Deacon was a performance artist. His performances typically focused on the production of an object. By 1974, however, the object itself became his primary interest, and he made the transition to the more tangible medium of sculpture. Deacon spent 1978–79 in the United States with his wife, who had a year-long fellowship in ceramics in New York. He discontinued making sculpture for the year and instead he drew and made pots, inspired by the German poet Rainer Maria Rilke's *Sonnets to Orpheus*. Deacon's work in these other mediums led him to his mature sculptural style, which is characterized by organically shaped, labor-intensive constructions that emphasize their manual fabrication. Typically, Deacon uses hand tools rather than prefabricated materials to produce his constructions. After making the short list for the Turner Prize in 1984, Deacon finally was awarded it in 1987. That same year, his work was brought to the attention of the American public by the exhibition *A Quiet Revolution: British Sculpture Since 1968*, at the Museum of Contemporary Art in Chicago.

Reference *Richard Deacon*. Pittsburgh: The Carnegie Museum of Art, 1988.

CARROLL DUNHAM (pp. 32–33)

Born 1949, New Haven, Connecticut
Studied Trinity College, Hartford, Connecticut, B.A., 1972
Resides New York

Carroll Dunham's introduction to the professional art world took place through an undergraduate semester spent as Dorothea Rockburne's studio assistant in New York, where he returned upon his graduation from college in 1972. He had his first solo exhibition in 1981 at the Artists Space in New York, and has since shown his work in numerous galleries, including the Jablonka Galerie in Cologne and the Sonnabend and Nolan/Eckman Galleries in New York. Dunham's distaste for the celebrity chic of the 1980s art world kept his work in the shadows of many of his better known contemporaries, although from the start, his paintings, drawings, and prints have received considerable critical attention. As a result, his work has appeared in numerous group exhibitions, including the 1991 and 1995 Whitney Biennials.

In the early 1980s, Dunham began using wood and wood veneers as supports for his work. In these paintings and drawings, he responded to the grain of the woods, both emulating and embellishing the striations of the grains to create the organically inspired forms that characterize his work. By 1989, Dunham shifted his work to canvas and paper and further experimented upon these surfaces with the shapes common to the woodgrain pictures. Although Dunham had studied photography and screenprinting at Trinity College, his first real foray into the production of multiples began in 1984, when United Limited Art Editions delivered a lithographic stone for him to experiment with. Since then, Dunham has produced numerous lithographic, intaglio, and relief editions.

References *Carroll Dunham: Drawings 1988–1991*. New York: David Nolan Gallery, 1992.

Carroll Dunham: Paintings and Drawings. Introduction by Dan Cameron. Cologne: Jablonka Galerie; New York: Sonnabend Gallery, 1990.

GÜNTHER FÖRG (pp. 34–35)

Born 1952, Füssen, West Germany
Studied Akademie der bildenden Künste, Munich, 1973–79
Resides Areuse, Switzerland

Since 1973, when he starting making large, monochromatic paintings, Günther Förg has dramatically diversified his oeuvre. In addition to the sizable canvases he still produces, Förg also casts bronze relief sculpture, takes photographs, makes prints, and constructs installations employing elements from all these different mediums. His work is rooted in Suprematism and Constructivism, but the impact of New York School painters like Barnett Newman and Brice Marden is also apparent, as is the influence of 1960s minimalism, notably in its German manifestations as articulated by Blinky Palermo. Like Newman's, much of Förg's work is produced as series, with similar objects all intended to be viewed together. Förg has also created bodies of work for particular exhibition spaces, such as a 1988 installation in the Gemeentemuseum in The Hague. This practice of producing work for a particular space underscores Förg's pronounced interest in the interplay between art objects and architecture. His work was featured in the 1992 *Documenta IX*, and he has had solo exhibitions at the Newport Harbor Art Museum and at the Museum Boymans–van Beuningen in Rotterdam.

Reference *Günther Förg: Gesamte Editionen / The Complete Editions, 1974–1988*. Essays by Luise Horn and Karel Schampers. Stuttgart: Edition Cantz, 1989.

FRANZ GERTSCH (pp. 36–37)

Born 1930, Mörigen, Switzerland
Studied Max von Mühlenen School, Bern, 1947–50
Resides Rüschegg-Heubach, Switzerland

Franz Gertsch was raised in a small town near Bern, Switzerland. The son of a schoolmaster and singer of lieder who encouraged his artistic inclinations, Gertsch studied painting at an art academy in Bern. In the late 1960s, after years of struggling with stylistic issues, he began to make paintings from photographic images projected onto canvases. For the most part, he used friends, family, and acquaintances from the art world as the subjects of these works. In 1980, he started to focus on his models' heads as his primary subject of representation. These facial portraits were often of monumental size, like the works of Chuck Close, to whom Gertsch is frequently compared. In 1986, Gertsch largely abandoned painting in favor of printmaking. Instead of projecting slides onto canvas, he projected his images onto sheets of wood, carving out his pictures instead of painting them. During a trip to Japan in 1987, Gertsch discovered sheets of handmade paper and pigments that were compatible with his conception of these woodcuts. Although in recent years Gertsch has ventured into landscape as a subject of his work, many of the first woodcuts were large-scale portraits not unlike the paintings that he had made in the early 1980s. In 1990, Gertsch had a solo exhibition of his woodcuts at the Museum of Modern Art in New York, and in 1991 at the Hirshhorn Museum in Washington. His early work was shown at the 1972 *Documenta 5* in Kassel and at the Venice Biennale in 1978.

References Rainer Michael Mason. *Franz Gertsch: Large-Scale Woodcuts*. Geneva: Cabinet des Estampes, 1990.

Franz Gertsch—Holzschnitte. Baden-Baden: Staatliche Kunsthalle, 1994.

KATHY GROVE (pp. 38–39)

Born 1948, Pittsburgh, Pennsylvania
Studied Rhode Island School of Design, B.F.A., 1970
Atelier 17, Paris, 1971–72
University of Wisconsin, Madison, M.A., 1975; M.F.A, 1976
Resides New York

By manipulating well-known imagery, Kathy Grove endeavors to make her audience recognize the diminished role that women have played, both within history and within the history of visual culture. In her photographic reproductions of famous paintings, prints, and photographs from throughout history, Grove either alters the appearance of female figures or removes them altogether. Her awareness of the manipulation of women within visual culture is also evident from her work with the Heresies Collective, a feminist collective concerned with art and politics.

Grove's work is often accomplished with the aid of a computer, and in 1994, Grove participated, with a team of specialists in computer-manipulated imagery, on a project meant to question perceptions of race. Benetton, a corporation known for its advocacy of multiculturalism and diversity, appealed to Site One New York, a computer imaging studio, to change the racial features of celebrities. The results included disconcerting photographs of Arnold Schwarzenegger as a black man and Spike Lee as a white man.

Grove has had solo exhibitions at Locks Gallery in Philadelphia and at the University Art Museum at California State University, Long Beach. She has also participated in exhibitions at the Museum of Modern Art in New York, the Houston Center for Photography, and the National Museum of American Art in Washington.

Reference *Kathy Grove: The Presence of Absence*. Essay by Constance W. Glenn. Long Beach: University Art Museum, California State University at Long Beach, 1992.

RICK MCKEE HOCK (pp. 40–41)

Born 1947, Nebraska
Studied University of Connecticut, Storrs, B.F.A., 1977
Visual Studies Workshop, State University of New York, Buffalo, M.F.A., 1979
Teaches School of Photographic Arts and Sciences, Rochester Institute of Technology
Resides Rochester, New York

After completing his M.F.A., Rick Hock began working at the International Museum of Photography at George Eastman House in Rochester, New York, where he is currently the Director of Creative Services. He is also an adjunct faculty member at the Rochester Institute of Technology, teaching classes in both black-and-white and color photography. In addition to his museum and teaching jobs, Hock has always managed to pursue his own photographic work. In the late 1970s, he used an 8-by-10-inch view camera to take landscape photographs of Rochester and the surrounding area. The open fields outside the city reminded him of the landscape of his childhood in Nebraska.

Hock's more recent work is less conventional and is informed by his job at the museum and by his familiarity with the history of visual culture. Called the *Codex* series, the works combine historical images and images from popular culture. The vast collection of the George Eastman House provides in part the material for these assemblages of photographic transfers of preexisting images. Using a variety of sources ranging from photographs in the museum's collection to pictures from art history textbooks, television, advertising, and trading cards, Hock typically takes 35-mm slides of the images and then makes 8-by-10-inch prints from the slides using Polaroid 809 color print material and an 81-12 film processor. These prints are then transferred in a grid pattern to Arches watercolor paper by laying the chemistry matrix face down on the paper and burnishing it with a spoon. By reconfiguring the individual images, Hock creates new contexts and meanings for them. In 1991, the Hartnett Gallery at the University of Rochester and the Denver Art Museum mounted solo exhibitions of Hock's work. He has also received two photographer's fellowships from the National Endowment for the Arts.

Reference Susan E. Cohen and William Johnson. "Interview with Rick Hock, October 31, 1991." *The Consort* [Rochester, N.Y.: International Museum of Photography at George Eastman House], December 1991, pp. 1–21.

PETER HUTCHINSON (pp. 42–43)

Born 1930, London
Studied University of Illinois, B.F.A., 1960
Resides Provincetown, Massachusetts

Although Peter Hutchinson was born in London, he was raised in a small, rural village in southeastern England near Margate. His country childhood fostered a strong interest in plants and gardening, and he went to college intending to pursue a degree in plant genetics. By the end of his first year at the University of Illinois, however, he had changed the focus of his study to art. His interest in nature, however, did not subside with his vocational change. Upon moving to New York in 1961, he was introduced to environmental works. By the time Hutchinson had his first solo exhibition at the John Gibson Gallery in 1969, he had forsaken abstract painting and was representing the natural world in his photographic collages and constructions. Immersion in and interaction with the environment are important to Hutchinson's work. For instance, in 1970, he engaged in an "action" (his preferred label for conceptually oriented work that lacks an audience), on the Parícutin volcano in Mexico, where he cultivated organic matter in order to demonstrate the tenacity of the living world. As with many of his other projects, he documented the undertaking with photographs and a written text. In 1976, after more than a decade of living in New York and traveling the world with his camera, Hutchinson moved to Provincetown, Massachusetts, where he still lives, works, and maintains a garden registered with the National Wildlife Federation. He continues to make environmental installations and photographic collages as well as publish books that combine his interests in photography, language, and gardening. Hutchinson has been the recipient of an NEA Fellowship and a DAAD Fellowship in Berlin.

Reference *The Narrative Art of Peter Hutchinson: A Retrospective.* Essays by Brian O'Doherty and Ann Wilson Lloyd. Provincetown, Mass.: Provincetown Arts Press, 1994.

ANISH KAPOOR (pp. 44–45)

Born 1954, Bombay, India
Studied Hornsey College of Art, London, 1973–77
Chelsea School of Art, London, 1977–78
Resides London

Born in India to a Hindu father and a Jewish mother, Anish Kapoor started college in Israel with the intention of studying engineering. In 1973, however, he moved to London in order to attend Hornsey College of Art. Since then, aside from brief visits to India, he has continued to live and work in London. After finishing his postgraduate work at the Chelsea School of Art, Kapoor returned to India in 1979 for the first time in seven years. While he was there, the piles of raw pigment sold by merchants for ritualistic and cosmetic purposes caught his attention. Upon his return to London, he began to incorporate pure, powdered pigment into his sculptural work. He first used it in conjunction with chalk powder in largely impermanent installation pieces. Two years later, he began using the brilliantly colored pigments (the primary colors, plus black and white) to cover solid materials such as wood, fiberglass, cement, and stone, that he fashioned into basic geometric shapes. The solid supports made his work more durable and allowed him to preserve the objects he made for future incorporation in sculptural groups. Because of his use of cheap materials in unconventional ways, his work has been frequently associated with Arte Povera, an influential Italian art movement of the 1960s that coincided with the establishment of minimalism in the United States.

Known primarily as a sculptor, although he has drawn continuously throughout his career, Kapoor represented Great Britain in the 1990 Venice Biennale. He won the Turner Prize in 1991, which is awarded by the Tate Gallery to a British artist under the age of fifty who has had an exemplary exhibition in the previous year. In 1992, Kapoor participated in *Documenta IX* in Kassel, and the Museum of Contemporary Art, San Diego, organized a show of his work that traveled to Des Moines, Ottawa, and Toronto.

References *Anish Kapoor.* Introduction by Lynda Forsha. San Diego: Museum of Contemporary Art, San Diego, 1992.

Jeremy Lewison. *Anish Kapoor: Drawings.* London: Tate Gallery, 1990.

MEL KENDRICK (pp. 46–47)

Born 1949, Boston
Studied Trinity College, Hartford, Connecticut, B.A., 1971
Hunter College, New York, M.A., 1973
Resides New York

Mel Kendrick's affinity for mathematics is apparent in his early sculptural work. His geometric constructions conform to the contemporary minimalist aesthetic established by artists like Carl Andre and Mel Bochner, artists Kendrick first encountered in Dorothea Rockburne's studio in New York. After receiving an M.A. from Hunter College in 1973, where he studied sculpture with Tony Smith and Robert Morris, Kendrick went to work in Rockburne's studio as her assistant. He credits Rockburne with introducing him to the New York art world. In 1980, his constructions were featured in a solo exhibition at John Weber Gallery, a renowned showplace for minimalist art during the 1970s. Over the course of the 1980s, Kendrick's sculptural forms strayed from the rigidly geometric shapes and austere materials typical of minimalism and became more organic. These later, large, freestanding sculptures for which Kendrick is best known are primarily made of wood that he has chopped, chain-sawed, painted, and reassembled, using the materials, tools, and working methods that he employs in his work as a building contractor. Although much of his sculpture is the result of putting an electric saw to wood, he laments the brutality of the technique. His work has been featured in exhibitions at the Saint Louis Art Museum, the Whitney Museum of American Art, and the Metropolitan Museum of Art. In 1990, Kendrick took a hiatus from his annual New York/Los Angeles alternating exhibition schedule in order to reevaluate his work and experiment with other mediums, such as drawing and printmaking. The large-scale, black-oil drawings shown at the Weatherspoon Art Gallery at the University of North Carolina at Greensboro in 1992 were an outcome of this period of experimentation.

Reference *Mel Kendrick: Black-Oil Sculpture and Drawing 1991–92.* Essay by Trevor Richardson. Greensboro: Weatherspoon Art Gallery, The University of North Carolina at Greensboro, 1992.

MARCIA KOCOT (pp. 48–49)

Born 1944, Northampton, Massachusetts
Studied Pennsylvania Academy of the Fine Arts, Philadelphia, C.F.A., 1967
University of Pennsylvania, B.F.A., 1987
Resides Philadelphia

THOMAS HATTON

Born 1946, Kingston, Pennsylvania
Studied Pennsylvania Academy of the Fine Arts, C.F.A., 1968
Resides Philadelphia

Over the past twenty-five years, the two artists now known as Kocot and Hatton have gone by a variety of names, including Tom Hatten and Xochital, Hatten Co., Tom and X Hatten, and Xochitaltomhatten. In the early years, only Hatton's name was associated with their work because it was often difficult to garner interest in collaborative projects. Kocot and Hatton met in 1964 when they were students at the Pennsylvania Academy of the Fine Arts, were married in 1967, and began working together during those years. Notably, the first work they ever sold to a museum was purchased by the Philadelphia Museum of Art in 1968. They are best known for the long-term portrait project they commenced in 1973, when they committed to painting weekly portraits of themselves over a ten-year period. They began the project using a palette of only black and white and added a new color each year, culminating in the addition of red in 1983. These portraits were intended to reveal the continuously changing social guises the two assumed. A sampling of these paintings was first exhibited in 1974, in the *Made in Philadelphia 2* show at the Institute of Contemporary Art. A number of the works also appeared in the opening exhibition of the Nexus Gallery in 1976, where as a pair, Kocot and Hatton were part of the original artists' cooperative. Since then, they have had solo exhibitions, including one entitled *Scale/Ratio: A Work for Two Sites*, shown at the Jessica Berwind Gallery and at the Levy Gallery for the Arts, at the Moore College of Art and Design in Philadelphia. Kocot and

Hatton's longstanding collaboration has inspired them to investigate other collaborative artistic efforts. Their research on the subject appeared in the 1990 catalogue of the exhibition *Team Spirit*, an examination of cooperative artistic projects. In 1995, Kocot and Hatton participated in the exhibition *Hiroshima: From Me to You*, at the Fukuya Gallery in Hiroshima. The show traveled to Tokyo and to other venues in the United States.

SHERRIE LEVINE (pp. 50–51)

Born 1947, Hazleton, Pennsylvania
Studied University of Wisconsin, Madison, B.F.A., 1969; M.F.A., 1973
Resides New York

Sherrie Levine garnered her first public and critical attention in 1981, when her *After Walker Evans* photographs were exhibited at Metro Pictures in New York. Hung on the gallery walls were newly matted and framed photographs of published reproductions of Evans's photographs, without any alterations made to the images. By presenting photographs of these well-known images as her own work, Levine challenged established notions of artistic originality and called into question the nature of appropriation, an endeavor she continues to pursue.

Levine was introduced to these artistic and theoretical concerns in 1975, when she moved to New York after living for two years on the West Coast. Within this environment, she met other young artists and critics and started reading psychoanalytic and film theory, both of which helped her formulate her ideas on the nature of representation. In the early 1980s, Levine made watercolors and casein paintings of other artists' work, continuing the same reproductive strategy she initiated in the earlier photographs. Since the mid-1980s, however, she has explored other types of representation, including stripe paintings and paintings of game boards. The chess and backgammon paintings refer to Marcel Duchamp's interest in games and thus, like her appropriations, situate her within a genealogy of artists. In recent years, Levine has employed the computer to re-represent the work of other artists, as is evidenced in her earlier series of paintings, also entitled *Meltdown*, in which she reduces well-known paintings to monochromatic fields.

Since 1981, Levine has been the object of copious critical attention, and her work has been featured in numerous exhibitions. The Kunsthalle in Zurich organized a retrospective of her work in 1991, and in 1993, continuing her appropriations, Levine fashioned glass likenesses of Constantin Brancusi's marble sculpture *Newborn* for an installation at the Philadelphia Museum of Art.

Reference *Sherrie Levine*. Essay by David Deitcher and interview by Jeanne Siegel. Zurich: Kunsthalle Zurich, 1991.

KATE MORAN (pp. 52–53)

Born 1958, Langhorne, Pennsylvania
Studied Antioch College, Yellow Springs, Ohio, B.F.A., 1982
Pennsylvania Academy of the Fine Arts, Philadelphia, Certificate, 1988
University of North Carolina at Chapel Hill, M.F.A., 1992
Resides Philadelphia

Even though Kate Moran studied ceramics at Antioch College and painting at the Pennsylvania Academy of the Fine Arts, in recent years she has worked primarily with photography and sculpture. While working on her M.F.A. at Chapel Hill, she began exploring these and other mediums, and since then has constructed installations, reworked photographs, made books, and worked with metal. It was also during graduate school that Moran was introduced to literary theory. While it is often assumed that her work is based on personal experiences, many of her ideas are derived from the theoretical texts she read at Chapel Hill and continues to read.

In recent years, Moran has been awarded a Pew Fellowship in the Arts and a Pennsylvania Council on the Arts Fellowship, as well as having had numerous solo exhibitions. In 1994, her photographs were exhibited at the More Gallery in Philadelphia, and an installation called *Nine Dolls Full of Color Who Understand Touch* was featured at the Philadelphia Art Alliance. The following year, a diverse sampling of her books, photographs, sculpture, and installation pieces was shown at the Williams Center for the Arts at Lafayette College.

Reference *Kate Moran: The Grotesque and Ideal*. Essay by Paula Marincola. Easton, Pa.: Williams Center for the Arts, Lafayette College, 1995.

RAYMOND PETTIBON (pp. 54–55)

Born 1957, Tucson, Arizona
Studied University of California at Los Angeles, B.A., 1977
Resides Hermosa Beach, California

As an undergraduate at UCLA, Raymond Pettibon studied economics, not art. He got his start as a professional artist the year after he graduated from college, when the band Black Flag used one of his drawings on an album jacket. He has since designed numerous record covers for a variety of rock groups, including Sonic Youth. Pettibon's early work for the hard rock music industry, as well as his creation of a highly regarded comic book, garnered him cult hero status in the southern California underground culture of the late 1970s and 1980s. In recent years, his work has attracted the attention of the more conventional art establishment.

Pettibon's work consists primarily of simple pen and wash drawings, accompanied by textual inscriptions. The inscriptions are conflations of preexisting texts and Pettibon's own musings and do not necessarily comment upon the images they accompany. During the 1980s, Pettibon assembled compilations of these drawings and issued them in small, photocopied editions. Besides producing books, he has also made videos, which have been screened at venues as diverse as the Museum of Modern Art and The Kitchen in New York. His work was shown in the 1993 Whitney Biennial, and in 1995 the Kunsthalle in Bern organized a solo exhibition of his drawings.

Reference *Raymond Pettibon*. Edited by Ulrich Loock. Bern: Kunsthalle; Paris: 14/16 Verneuil, 1995.

JUDY PFAFF (pp. 56–57)

Born 1946, London
Studied Washington University, Saint Louis, B.F.A., 1971
Yale University, New Haven, Connecticut, M.F.A., 1973
Teaches Columbia University, New York
Resides New York

Judy Pfaff was born in postwar London in 1946 and moved to Michigan with her family in 1959. It was there that her talents were detected by a teacher, and she was enrolled in a Detroit high school for artistically gifted children. Although Pfaff is known primarily as a sculptor, she took only one sculpture class in art school and considers her mentor to be the painter Al Held. All through school Pfaff painted large, colorful, abstract canvases. In 1973, however, she stopped painting altogether and started making small objects. She subsequently learned welding and other metal and woodworking skills, which prepared her to make the large-scale installations for which she is best known. Pfaff's installations have been likened to landscapes, both actual and metaphorical. *Deepwater*, the installation that brought her celebrity in 1980, was inspired by the underwater environment she encountered while snorkeling in the Caribbean, although the piece is not intended to be a replica of an underwater scene. Like her paintings, these installations are composed of many bright colors, the hues meant to evoke an otherworldly atmosphere. In the mid-1980s, Pfaff found her installations increasingly difficult to disassemble and abandon and almost impossible to sell. She began to focus on more permanent constructions, such as three-dimensional wall sculptures, and started shying away from temporary site installations. Currently a professor at Columbia, Pfaff has supported herself by teaching at various institutions, including Yale and the School of Visual Arts, New York. Her work has been shown in solo exhibitions at the Saint Louis Art Museum, the Hirshhorn Museum in Washington, and the Fabric Workshop in Philadelphia. In 1989, the National Museum of Women in the Arts featured her work in their series on young women artists, and in 1995, Pfaff created a permanent installation for the Pennsylvania Convention Center in Philadelphia.

Reference *Judy Pfaff: 10,000 Things/ Forefront*. Essays by Linda Nochlin and Helaine Posner. New York: Holly Solomon Gallery; Washington, D.C.: National Museum of Women in the Arts, 1988.

MARKUS RAETZ (pp. 58–59)

Born 1941, Büren an der Aare, Switzerland
Studied L'École Normale de Hofwil, 1957–61
Resides Bern, Switzerland

Markus Raetz began his artistic career in the early 1960s drawing comic strips, and his fidelity to line drawings has persisted over three decades. Over the years, Raetz has filled numerous notebooks with sketches that sometimes evolve into more resolved drawings and other times remain fanciful doodlings that provide insight into his other work. His oeuvre is not restricted to particular subjects or mediums. He has produced both figural and abstract subjects, as well as landscapes, in mediums as various as photography, printmaking, drawing, sculpture, and installation, and these works have appeared in diverse international venues. In 1988, Raetz represented Switzerland in the Venice Biennale and has since had numerous solo exhibitions, including those at the Museum of Contemporary Art, San Diego, the New Museum of Contemporary Art in New York, and the Cabinet des Estampes in Geneva.

Much of Raetz's work is concerned with an examination of the senses, especially sight and touch. He has repeatedly represented the act of seeing, such as in drawings portraying emanations from the eyes, images which seemingly picture vision. His images of touch analogously portray hands holding different objects. Raetz's work, however, is not limited to the representation of sensation but also explores the means of perception. He is well known for his anamorphic drawings and constructions, images which are only recognizable from a singular viewing position.

References Rainer Michael Mason and Juliane Willi-Cosandier. *Markus Raetz: Les Estampes, Die Druckgraphik, The Prints, 1958–1991*. Geneva: Cabinet des Estampes, 1991.

Markus Raetz. Essay by Max Wechsler. Valencia: IVAM Centre Julio González, 1993.

GERHARD RICHTER (pp. 60–61)

Born 1932, Dresden, East Germany
Studied Kunstakademie, Dresden, 1951–56
Staatlichen Kunstakademie, Düsseldorf, 1961–63
Teaches Staatlichen Kunstakademie, Düsseldorf
Resides Cologne

Two months before the Berlin Wall was erected, Gerhard Richter left Dresden to study in Düsseldorf. He had already spent five years studying painting at the Kunstakademie in Dresden, but felt oppressed there by the imposition of the official Social Realist style. Seeing Jackson Pollock's work at the 1959 *Documenta II* in Kassel fostered his desire to study modernist modes of representation, and so in 1961, he relocated to Düsseldorf. Intent on remaining a practitioner of the traditional medium of painting and yet also determined to exercise a modernist approach, Richter began making paintings of photographic images in 1962. The photographs were collected from sources as diverse as the news media and snapshots from family albums. In 1966, he began taking his own photographs during his travels, which became the models for his painted landscapes. Satisfied with these "photo paintings," Richter destroyed most of his earlier work. He has continued to paint photographic images projected onto canvases, adding landscape, mountain, and city views to his inventory of subjects.

Throughout Richter's career, his work has become increasingly eclectic. In the late 1960s, he did a series of color charts, painting swatches of assorted colors on canvases. For the 1972 Venice Biennale, he painted *Forty-eight Portraits*, depictions in black and white of notable figures from modern history. In 1976, Richter turned to extremely gestural and highly colorful abstract paintings. In 1988, he made a series of grisaille paintings from media photographs related to the 1977 suicides of three imprisoned members of a West German terrorist group. In recent years, he has continued to make both figurative and abstract paintings utilizing photographic sources.

Richter has meticulously documented his work since his photo paintings of 1962. After the completion of each work, he assigns it a number and adds it to a list. He has also compiled a compendium of his photographic sources, which presently consists of thousands of photographs affixed to panels. This collection, called "Atlas," has been the subject of a number of exhibitions, while his "picture index" has been published as a lithograph. In 1993–94, a retrospective of Richter's work traveled to the Musée d'Art Moderne de la Ville de Paris, the Kunst- und Ausstellungshalle der Bundesrepublik Deutschland in Bonn, the Moderna Museet in Stockholm, and the Museo Nacional Centro de Arte Reina Sofía in Madrid.

Reference *Gerhard Richter*. 3 vols. Bonn: Kunst- und Ausstellungshalle der Bundesrepublik Deutschland, 1993.

EDWARD RUSCHA (pp. 62–63)

Born 1937, Omaha, Nebraska
Studied Chouinard Art Institue, Los Angeles, 1956–60
Resides Venice, California

Although Ed Ruscha is considered a California artist, he was born in Omaha, Nebraska, and raised in Oklahoma City. Ruscha didn't settle on the West Coast until 1956, when he moved to Los Angeles to attend art school. Taking his father's practical advice, he made plans to study commercial art and enrolled at the Chouinard Institute in Los Angeles, a local training ground for Disney illustrators. The school also specialized in the fine arts, and there Ruscha was exposed to some of the best contemporary artists in the city. When he left the school in 1960, he began working for an advertising agency and subsequently had a number of other short-lived jobs as a commercial artist, including hand decorating ceramic denture holders and designing layouts for *Artforum*. In the wake of these experiences, Ruscha resolved to dedicate himself to his own work and has since become an iconic figure on the West Coast art scene.

In the early 1960s, Ruscha began making paintings of commercial sites and logos. His fascination with the contemporary symbols and landscape of the American southwest and southern California is apparent in these early paintings, as well as in his first book, *Twenty-six Gasoline Stations*, of 1963. Three years later, he published the book *Every Building on the Sunset Strip*, and in 1968 he made a screenprint of the "Hollywood" sign. During these years, he also made paintings of words against monochromatic and figurative backgrounds. Throughout the 1970s, Ruscha used rather unusual materials in a number of these works. Substances such as gunpowder, egg yolk, ketchup, and berry juices were employed to render the words and phrases on paper, canvas, or fabric. Ruscha has continued to paint words in recent years, although sometimes they are forsaken for empty white bands designating their absence. In 1982, the San Francisco Museum of Modern Art organized a retrospective of Ruscha's paintings, drawings, prints, and books. He has since had solo exhibitions at the Museum of Contemporary Art, Los Angeles, and at the Whitney Museum of American Art in New York.

Reference *The Works of Edward Ruscha*. Essays by Dave Hickey and Peter Plagens. New York: Hudson Hills Press in association with the San Francisco Museum of Modern Art, 1982.

ALISON SAAR (pp. 64–65)

Born Los Angeles, 1956
Studied Scripps College, Claremont, California, B.A., 1978
Otis Art Institute, Los Angeles, M.F.A., 1981
Resides Brooklyn, New York

Alison Saar's work combines the forms and themes of both African American traditions and modern black experience. Her interest in the evolution of African magic and ritual, from its preslave trade roots to its manifestation in modern urban settings, is evident in the mythologized figures and environments she creates. She incorporates found objects into her work—bits of wood, metal, and ceramic—intrigued by the lost histories of the objects. This practice is emblematic of her whole enterprise. By recreating traditional forms and figures, she attempts to reinvent their lost meaning and history. Her interest in the preservation of traditional iconography is also evident in her studies as an art history major at Scripps College, where she investigated African influences on various aspects of art and wrote her senior thesis on black American folk art.

Although most of Saar's two-dimensional and sculptural work is figurative, she never studied life drawing while in school; as a graduate student, she concentrated mostly on abstract representations. She credits her father, a conservator of art, with teaching her many of the technical skills necessary for making the kind of carved, mixed-media figures and installation pieces that she now creates. As an unofficial apprentice to him during her school years, she learned how to carve and construct objects as they worked together on mummies and on African and pre-Columbian artifacts. Saar's mother, Betye Saar, is also an artist of considerable stature, and in 1990, UCLA's Wight Art Gallery organized a joint exhibition of their work. Since then, Saar has had solo exhibitions at the Hirshhorn Museum and Sculpture Garden in Washington, D.C., and at the High Museum of Art in Atlanta. One of her works also appeared in the 1993 Whitney Biennial, and in 1995, she erected a temporary installation piece in the lobby of the Brooklyn Museum.

Reference *Secrets, Dialogues and Revelation: The Art of Betye and Alison Saar*. Edited by Elizabeth Shepherd. Los Angeles: Wight Art Gallery, University of California, 1990.

KIKI SMITH (pp. 66–67)

Born 1954, Nuremberg, West Germany
Studied Hartford Art School
Resides New York

Kiki Smith was raised in New Jersey within a family where artistic expression flourished—her grandfather was an altar carver; her father, the sculptor Tony Smith; her mother, an actress and singer; and her sister, an artist. Smith grew up helping her father with his work and also studied briefly at the Hartford Art School. Her varied studies in other areas also inform her work. Besides a year at a vocational school to learn industrial baking, Smith later trained as an emergency medical technician in New York for a few months in 1985. Smith's EMT training was prompted by her fascination with the human body as a subject of representation. She is not interested in depicting the idealized body, but the body as a functional organism, full of bones, fluids, and organs that sometimes break down. Since 1979, when Smith used *Gray's Anatomy* as a source for her anatomical imagery, her use of the human body has become more immediate and personal, and in recent years she has incorporated her own body into her art. Although Smith's primary medium has been paper in a variety of guises, she has also fabricated pieces using such diverse materials as cloth, wax, glass, wood, and ceramic.

By the time Smith was invited to make prints at Universal Limited Art Editions in 1989, her work had been included in many major group exhibitions. In recent years, she has also had numerous solo exhibitions, including shows at the Museum of Modern Art in New York and the Corcoran Gallery of Art in Washington, though she did not begin her career by exhibiting in such traditional venues. In the late 1970s, Smith belonged to Collaborative Projects, Inc. (COLAB), a politically oriented artists' collective that presented its work in unconventional spaces. COLAB's "Times Square Show" of 1980 was the site of Smith's first exhibition of body-derived art, as well as her introduction to printmaking. Smith learned to silkscreen in order to make T-shirts to sell in conjunction with the show. She remains attentive to pressing social concerns, like gender issues and the AIDS epidemic.

Reference *Kiki Smith: Prints and Multiples, 1985–1993*. Boston: Barbara Krakow Gallery, 1994.

PAUL THEK (pp. 68–69)

Born 1933, Brooklyn, New York
Studied Art Students League, New York, 1950
Pratt Institute, Brooklyn, 1950
Cooper Union School of Art, New York, 1951–54
Died 1988, New York

Although Paul Thek was a well-known figure in the New York art world of the early 1960s, he moved to Europe in 1962, and the work that he did there over the next fifteen years was little known in the United States. It was hoped that the 1977 exhibition *Processions* at the Institute of Contemporary Art in Philadelphia would rekindle interest in his work in his native country, but substantial recognition of its significance did not come until after the artist's death from AIDS in 1988.

In the early 1960s, Thek was known in New York for his "technological reliquaries," realistic wax representations of raw meat encased in sleek plexiglass boxes. A participant in the American counterculture of the 1960s, he opposed the styles and trends of contemporary art, renouncing what he viewed as the commercialism of Pop Art and the emptiness of minimalism. His aversion to the current American situation instigated his flight to Europe in the mid-1960s, where he divided his time between Ponza, an island off the coast of Naples, and Amsterdam.

With the creation of the installation *The Tomb—Death of a Hippie* in 1967, Thek embarked on the production of a series of environments installed in galleries, most notably *The Procession / The Artist's Co-op*, produced for Amsterdam's Stedelijk Museum and *Pyramid / A Work in Progress*, created at the Moderna Museet in Stockholm. Thek's interest in creating broadly encompassing installation pieces seems to have stemmed from his Roman Catholic background, which stimulated his fascination with sacred spaces and ritual. He called his environments "processions," in part as a wordplay upon the process of making art, and in part because many of the same objects were reused and reconfigured in each installation, giving them a ritualistic, almost sanctified aspect. Thek utilized found objects in these environments, including newspapers, cast-off junk, and even a latex dwarf.

References *Paul Thek / Processions*. Philadelphia: Institute of Contemporary Art, University of Pennsylvania, 1977.

Holland Carter. "Thek's Social Reliquaries." *Art in America*, June 1990, pp. 132ff.

ROSEMARIE TROCKEL (pp. 70–71)

Born 1952, Schwerte, West Germany
Studied Werkkunstschule, Cologne, 1974–78
Resides Cologne

Rosemarie Trockel's marginalization within the male-dominated Rhineland artists' collective Mülheimer Freiheit was in part the inspiration for the formation of the Monika Sprüth Galerie in Cologne in the early 1980s. Trockel and her friend Sprüth wanted to create an exhibition space that would make the work of contemporary women artists more visible in Germany. The gallery, in cooperation with Trockel, also produced the magazine *Eau de Cologne* in the late 1980s with the same intention. The magazine's title is a play on Marcel Duchamp's conceptual piece, *Air de Paris*. Trockel has been called a third generation Duchampian, her work also having been informed by the second generation Duchampian artists Joseph Beuys, Sigmar Polke, and Andy Warhol.

Trockel first gained recognition in 1985 for her knit fabric works. Supposedly in response to a male art critic's comment that women were not capable of producing art but were better suited to weaving, she began making woven images. Because of this work and her association with the Sprüth Gallery, her work is often deemed feminist in character. It seems to defy such easy categorization, however, especially since Trockel does not do the weaving herself, but has the fabrics produced by computer-governed machines. Trockel's oeuvre is not limited to woven work and can only be characterized as heterogeneous, since she also draws, paints, sculpts, makes constructions, installations, and prints, and has recently begun to make videos. Her first solo exhibition was held in 1983 at the Galerie Philomene Magers in Bonn, and traveled to the Monika Sprüth Galerie; since then, her work has been featured in the *Projects Series* (1988) at the Museum of Modern Art in New York. The Institute of Contemporary Art in Boston and the University Art Museum at the University of California, Berkeley, have jointly organized a major retrospective of her work.

Reference *Rosemarie Trockel*. Edited by Sidra Stich. Munich: Prestel, 1991.

JAVIER VALLHONRAT (pp. 72–73)

Born 1953, Madrid
Studied Facultad de Bellas Artes, Universidad de Madrid, 1986
Resides Madrid

Besides working on his own photographic series, Javier Vallhonrat has worked as a fashion photographer for Condé Nast publications since 1984. Soon after starting a degree in painting at the Facultad de Bellas Artes in Madrid in 1972, he began working as an assistant to a photographer friend of his father's. He has since established himself as a fashion photographer of international acclaim and worked with some of the foremost fashion designers in Europe. His photographs have appeared in the Italian, British, and French editions of *Vogue* magazine. In 1981, he began a series of fine art photographs called *Homages*, and has subsequently produced a number of other series, including *The Possessed Space* (1987–91) and *Autograms* (1991). He earned a degree in fine arts from the University of Madrid in 1986. His work as a fashion photographer allows him to spend six months of every year on his own work.

Vallhonrat has had numerous solo exhibitions, including shows at Hamilton's Gallery in London and Galería Juana Mordó in Madrid. He also participated in the 1991 exhibition *Four Directions: Twenty Years of Contemporary Spanish Photography, 1970–1990*, at the Museo Nacional Centro de Arte Reina Sofía in Madrid, and in *Splendeurs et Misères du Corps*, at the Musée d'Art Moderne in Paris. He received Spain's National Photography Award for 1995.

References *Javier Vallhonrat: El Espacio Poseido* [The possessed space]. Essay by Manuel Santos Alguacil. Madrid: Signo Impresores, 1990.

Javier Vallhonrat: Autograms. Munich: Gina Kehayoff, 1993.

WILLIAM WEGMAN (pp. 74–75)

Born 1943, Holyoke, Massachusetts
Studied Massachusetts College of Art, Boston, B.F.A., 1965
University of Illinois, Champaign-Urbana, M.F.A., 1967
Resides New York

Although William Wegman is best known for his photographs of his two dogs, Man Ray and Fay Ray, he has always worked in a variety of mediums. After earning his M.F.A. from the University of Illinois in painting, Wegman made glow-in-the-dark minimalist sculpture, enacted environmental happenings with styrofoam, and in 1969, began making videos. The following year, he determined that staged photography, because of its predictability, was the most congenial medium for his ideas. That same year, Wegman also acquired a weimaraner named Man Ray, and because the dog was always underfoot, the artist decided that it was just easier to make him the subject of his video and photographic work. In 1979, the Polaroid Corporation invited Wegman to Cambridge, Massachusetts, to experiment with their large format camera, an invitation that resulted in the well-known series of 20-by-24-inch color prints of Man Ray. The dog died in 1982, and after several years without a pet or "artistic collaborator," Wegman adopted another dog, Fay Ray. Throughout, he continued to make videos and drawings, and in 1985, after a hiatus of nearly twenty years, Wegman began to paint again.

Because of the humorous nature of Wegman's work (as well as his statements), his work is sometimes dismissed as frivolous. But even the most comic dog photographs play on many of the more complex issues of postmodernist representation. Wegman is one of the foremost conceptual artists of his generation, and his work often incorporates complex visual and verbal puns. The theoretical complexity of Wegman's work, however, has not diminished its popular appeal. Wegman and his dogs have appeared on "The Tonight Show," "Saturday Night Live," and "Late Night with David Letterman," and since 1989, Wegman and Fay Ray have made numerous videos for "Sesame Street." The dogs' appeal to youthful audiences is also apparent from Wegman's photographic renditions of *Cinderella* and *Little Red Riding Hood*, in which costumed dogs play all the roles. Wegman's work has also been the subject of numerous museum and gallery exhibitions. In 1982, the Walker Art Center in Minneapolis held a retrospective entitled *Wegman's World*, and in 1990 the Kunstmuseum in Lucerne, Switzerland, organized a retrospective that traveled to various venues in Europe and the United States, culminating in 1992 with an exhibition at the Whitney Museum of American Art.

Reference *William Wegman: Paintings, Drawings, Photographs, Videotapes*. Edited by Martin Kunz. New York: Harry Abrams, 1990.

NEIL WINOKUR (pp. 76–77)

Born 1945, Queens, New York
Studied Hunter College, New York, B.A., 1967
Resides New York

Neil Winokur had his first solo exhibition at the Barbara Toll Gallery in New York in 1986. The work of his previous group exhibitions had consisted of oversized photographic portraits—only the sitter's heads and shoulders shown against unadorned, luridly colored backdrops. In the show at the Toll Gallery, however, Winokur expanded the parameters of his portrait photography. With each photograph of an individual (many of them were well-known figures from the art world, while others were dogs), he grouped photographs of objects chosen by the sitters as representative of their personal cosmologies. Significantly, these photographic assemblages, called "totems," were arranged in the shapes of crosses, pyramids, and totem poles.

The year 1990 marked a transition in Winokur's work. Instead of continuing to focus on the objects within his totemic constructions as biographical emblems of his models, he began to exhibit photographs of the objects by themselves. Like his portraits of people, the objects were photographed against the same brightly colored backgrounds. But Winokur's digression from biography was not absolute. That same year, he turned to autobiography and subjected himself to the same photographic treatment he had previously used for other sitters and their objects. In recent years, Winokur has had an exhibition featuring portraits of dogs, as well as a memorial exhibition for a friend who died of AIDS. In 1993, the Denver Art Museum held the first retrospective of his work. Rather than teaching or working in a photographic studio to supplement his own photography, Winokur has worked on and off for the last twenty years for the Strand bookstore in New York.

Reference *Everyday Things: Photographs by Neil Winokur.* Edited by Constance Sullivan. Washington, D.C.: Smithsonian Institution Press, 1994.

ROBIN WINTERS (pp. 78–79)

Born 1950, Benicia California
Studied San Francisco Art Institute, 1971
Whitney Independent Study Program, 1972–76
Resides New York

Robin Winters's social conciousness is apparent in his life and in his attitude toward art. The rebellious son of two prosperous lawyers, he quit high school at the age of sixteen, left home, and supported himself by working in factories. The personal significance of the time he spent as a blue-collar laborer is reflected in the fact that he still maintains his union memberships, and further, that he lists them on his résumé alongside his teaching stints and lectures at universities. Winters dislikes the competitive, market aspects of art production, and champions the social value of art—art as a forum to change and heal the world. He has worked toward this goal by participating in artistic collaborations, including performance pieces, videos, and writings, that focus on social and political issues. In 1977, along with several other artists, he helped found Collaborative Projects, Inc. (COLAB), and participated in their infamous 1980 "Times Square Show." Even though Winters contends that all of his work is political in nature, its social value is accompanied by witty and playful qualities. Winters has worked in a variety of mediums, ranging from performance and installation pieces to the more traditional forms of painting, printmaking, and glasswork. He has had solo exhibitions at the Institute of Contemporary Art in Boston and at the Wadsworth Atheneum in Hartford. His piece in the 1975 Whitney Biennial consisted of a continuous performance which entailed, in part, interviewing museum visitors while dressed as a bear.

Reference *Robin Winters: Thinktank*. Essays by David Ross and Roberta Smith. Boston: Institute of Contemporary Art, 1986.

CHRISTOPHER WOOL (pp. 80–81)

Born 1955, Chicago
Studied Sarah Lawrence College, New York, 1973
New York Studio School, 1974
New York University, 1978
Resides New York

Christopher Wool had his first solo exhibition in 1984 at the Cable Gallery in New York, where he exhibited a series of "poured" paintings. The following year, he began dripping layers of enamel paint onto sheets of aluminum mounted on wood. Although the drip method resonates of Jackson Pollock, the paintings do not have any of the gestural vitality of a painting by Pollock. The drips may have been randomly applied to the metallic surface, but their application was meticulous and thus gives the paintings a very ordered and patterned appearance that Pollock's paintings lack. Two years later, Wool abandoned the arbitrary application of paint and opted instead for a more mechanical method of image production. In order to maintain the repetitive aspect of the drip paintings, he began applying paint to the metal supports with an incised rubber roller, producing patterns of leaves, flowers, or vines. Stamping floral and figural motifs proved to achieve a similar effect. Although the designs of these images are repetitious, there are variations visible in each painting, such as splattered paint or misaligned registration, that make each a unique image.

At about the same time he began making the rolled and stamped floral and ornamental patterns, Wool also started making word paintings. In response to some graffiti he saw painted on the side of a white truck, he used stencils to inscribe black-lettered words on a smooth white background. The words are often missing vowels and split non-syllabically, so that they are difficult to immediately comprehend. They are always printed in capital letters, and their format as well as their content is frequently confrontational. He has used words such as TERRORIST, RIOT, and HYPOCRITE, all meant to disconcert the viewer of these large-scale works. Wool participated in the 1989 Whitney Biennial, as well as the 1992 *Documenta IX* in Kassel. He has also had solo exhibitions at the San Francisco Museum of Modern Art, the Kunstverein in Cologne, and the Luhring Augustine Gallery in New York. Wool has also produced numerous books, including *CATS IN BAG BAGS IN RIVER*, which was published in conjunction with an exhibition at the Museum Boymans–van Beuningen in Rotterdam.

Reference *New Work: Christopher Wool.* Essay by John Caldwell. San Francisco: San Francisco Museum of Modern Art, 1989.